Where to Next?
Travel and Tourism Communication

James Bury   Anthony Sellick   Kaori Horiuchi

photographs by
iStockphoto

音声ファイルのダウンロード／ストリーミング

CD マーク表示がある箇所は、音声を弊社 HP より無料でダウンロード／ストリーミングすることができます。下記 URL の書籍詳細ページに音声ダウンロードアイコンがございますのでそちらから自習用音声としてご活用ください。

https://www.seibido.co.jp/ad712

Where to Next? – Travel and Tourism Communication

Copyright © 2025 by James Bury, Anthony Sellick, Kaori Horiuchi

All rights reserved for Japan.
No part of this book may be reproduced in any form
without permission from Seibido Co., Ltd.

Preface

In today's global society it is becoming increasingly important to be able to communicate in a wide range of contexts. This includes talking about different topics, interacting with different people, expressing opinions, and justifying viewpoints.

Where to Next? – Travel and Tourism Communication is a new textbook that aims to develop students' overall communication skills, incorporating both receptive and productive activities.

Each of the fifteen units in the *Where to Next? – Travel and Tourism Communication* student book covers a specific topic that focuses on various contexts connected to travel and tourism. The topics range from Choosing a Vacation and Resolving Issues to Local Food and Shopping.

Each unit incorporates easy to follow activities that provide opportunities to learn and practice vocabulary as well as listening activities that focus on the gist and the details of the listening texts. Each unit also includes speaking activities that provide practice of the core language needed to interact effectively in pair conversations and small group discussions as well as pronunciation activities that focus on accuracy and understanding. Furthermore, each unit is accompanied by an activity in the appendix that encourages extended speaking and/or writing.

We hope that you will find the topics and activities interesting and thought-provoking, and that they encourage you to learn more about successful communication strategies and techniques, especially when traveling and/or encountering tourists. We sincerely hope you enjoy studying and working through *Where to Next? – Travel and Tourism Communication*.

James Bury, Anthony Sellick, and Kaori Horiuchi

EnglishCentralのご案内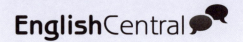

　本テキスト各ユニットの「I Vocabulary」のPart B、「II Listening and Speaking 1」、「V Listening and Speaking 2」と「VI Pronunciation」のExercise Bで学習する音声は、オンライン学習システム「EnglishCentral」で学習することができます。

　EnglishCentralでは動画の視聴や単語のディクテーションのほか、動画のセリフを音読し録音すると、コンピュータが発音を判定します。PCのwebだけでなく、スマートフォン、タブレットではアプリでも学習できます。リスニング、スピーキング、語彙力向上のため、ぜひ活用してください。

　EnglishCentralの利用にはアカウントとアクセスコードの登録が必要です。登録方法については下記ページにアクセスしてください。
（画像はすべてサンプルで、実際の教材とは異なります）

https://www.seibido.co.jp/englishcentral/pdf/ectextregister.pdf

見る

- 本文内でわからなかった単語は1クリックでその場で意味を確認
- スロー再生

学ぶ

- 音声を聴いて空欄の単語をタイピング。ゲーム感覚で楽しく単語を覚える

話す

- 動画のセリフを音読し録音、コンピュータが発音を判定。
- 日本人向けに専門開発された音声認識によってスピーキング力を％で判定
- ネイティブと自分が録音した発音を聞き比べ練習に生かすことができます
- 苦手な発音記号を的確に判断し、単語を緑、黄、赤の3色で表示

Contents

UNIT 1 *Where shall we go?* 6
- Choosing a Vacation

UNIT 2 *Just click there.* 12
- Booking a Vacation

UNIT 3 *Let's get ready.* 18
- Packing and Preparing

UNIT 4 *Which gate?* 24
- At the Airport (Departing)

UNIT 5 *Where are the taxis?* 30
- At the Airport (Arriving)

UNIT 6 *Welcome!* 36
- Checking In

UNIT 7 *This isn't right.* 42
- Resolving Problems

UNIT 8 *Let's work out.* 48
- Hotel Facilities and Services

UNIT 9 *Where's the station?* 54
- Getting Around Town

UNIT 10 *Look at that!* 60
- Sights and Tourist Spots

UNIT 11 *Why are they doing that?* 66
- Local Culture

UNIT 12 *It's delicious!* 72
- Local Food

UNIT 13 *I don't feel good.* 78
- Medicine and Health

UNIT 14 *How much is it?* 84
- Shopping

UNIT 15 *Where to next?* 90
- Reminiscing and Future Plans

Appendix 96

UNIT 01

Where shall we go?
Choosing a Vacation

I Vocabulary

A Match the English words and phrases (1~10) to the Japanese words (a~j).

1. ____ adventure
2. ____ cruise
3. ____ abroad
4. ____ sightseeing
5. ____ hot spring
6. ____ spend
7. ____ diving
8. ____ amazing
9. ____ local
10. ____ culture

| a. クルーズ | b. 冒険 | c. 温泉 | d. 過ごす | e. 海外へ |
| f. 文化 | g. 素晴らしい | h. 地元の | i. 潜水 | j. 観光 |

B Complete the dialogs with words and phrases from Part A. 1-02~06

1. **A:** What kind of vacation would you like to go on next?
   B: Hmm, maybe a(n) _____. I've never been on a ship before, so I'd like to try it.

2. **A:** What did you do on your last vacation?
   B: I went _____ around Kyoto. I saw lots of amazing places like Kiyomizudera and Kinkakuji.

6

3. **A:** What was the best vacation you've ever had?
   B: That's a tough question, but I'd have to say a trip to Thailand I went on four years ago. I went _____ and saw a turtle. It was awesome!

4. **A:** Where in your country should I go to learn about the traditional _____?
   B: You should definitely visit the British Museum. You can learn a lot about Britain and British history there.

5. **A:** Have you ever been _____?
   B: No, I haven't, I've only visited other places in Japan. I really would love to go to another country, though. It would be great, wouldn't it?

C Practice the dialogs in Part B with a partner.

D Now, ask your partner the questions in Part B. Give your own responses.

II Listening and Speaking 1   1-07

A Listen to the questions and write them below.

1. _____
2. _____
3. _____
4. _____

B Now, select the best responses from the choices below.

1. a. Yes, lots of times.   b. Yes, I do.   c. It's fun.
2. a. I went to Kyoto last year.   b. I'd like to go to Kyoto.   c. Is Kyoto nice?
3. a. I've never tried it.   b. I can do it.   c. Yes, I would.
4. a. I like warm places more.   b. It's warm today.   c. He is cool.

C Next, ask your partner the questions in Part A. Give your own responses.

III Listening

A Listen to two people talking about their vacations. Write the places they visited and check (O) the correct boxes.

1. Place: _____

	Yes	No
• went with friends		
• stayed in a hotel		
• went to the beach		
• would go back		

2. Place: _____

	Yes	No
• went with friends		
• stayed in a hotel		
• went to the beach		
• would go back		

B Listen to the speakers again. Complete the texts below.

Speaker 1

I went to Fukushima last year with two (1) _____. We stayed in a traditional Japanese hotel with a really great hot spring. It didn't take (2) _____ long to get there, just two and a half (3) _____, so not so bad. We stayed there for two nights and spent the whole time in the hotel. You might think that sounds boring, but it really wasn't. The food in the hotel (4) _____ was some of the best I've ever had. I'd (5) _____ go back again.

Speaker 2

I always go camping with my family. But this (1) _____ our trip was different. We went to (2) _____ country! We stayed for 10 days in Tuscany, Italy. Normally, we (3) _____ stay for that long, but I'm glad we did. The campsite was very close to the beach, so we spent a lot of time there, but we also spent time (4) _____ and exploring the local towns, too. We all had a great time, but I don't think I'd go back. I'd like to go (5) _____ different. Going to different places is best.

UNIT 1 | *Where shall we go?*

IV Speaking 1

Which of the following are important to you when choosing a vacation? Check the boxes below and talk to your partner about what they think.

	Very important	Quite important	Not important	Reason
• beautiful views	☐	☐	☐	
• traditional culture	☐	☐	☐	
• good food	☐	☐	☐	
• interesting places	☐	☐	☐	
• weather / climate	☐	☐	☐	
• _____	☐	☐	☐	
• _____	☐	☐	☐	

V Listening and Speaking 2

1-10

A Listen to the conversation and complete the text below.

Li: We have some time off from (1) _____ soon. Let's go somewhere.

Satoshi: Great (2) _____ ! Where shall we go?

Li: How about going to **Okinawa**? **The beaches** there are (3) _____ and we could go **diving**, too.

Satoshi: That would be nice, but I've been there (4) _____ _____ _____ times before. Why don't we go **abroad**?

Li: Well, we could go to **Egypt**. I've (5) _____ _____ _____ **go on an adventure** and we could definitely do that there!

Satoshi: Yes, we could (6) _____ _____ _____ *cruise down the River Nile*.

B Now, practice the conversation with a partner.

C Next, change the information in *italics* using your own ideas and practice again.

9

VI Pronunciation

【複数形の発音：/s/ /z/ /ɪz/】

数えられる名詞が複数の場合、語尾に -s や -es をつけます。単語によって末尾の発音が異なるので、注意する必要があります。例外もありますが、基本的な3つのパターンを覚えておきましょう。

1. -s, -es の前が無声子音［p, t, k, f, θ］で終わる場合は /s/ と発音します。日本語のスに近い音です。　例）stops /s/　nights /s/（ts で終わると繋げて「ツッ」のように発音します。）
2. -s, -es の前が母音または有声子音（b, d, g, n など声帯を振動させる音）で終わる場合は /z/ と発音します。日本語のズに近い音です。　例）towns /z/　cards /z/
3. -es の前が無声子音［s, z, ʃ, tʃ, dʒ, ʒ］で終わる場合は /ɪz/ と発音します。日本語のイズに近い音です。　例）places /ɪz/　buses /ɪz/

Exercises

A Listen to the words and choose the correct sound.　　1-11

1. /s/　/z/　/ɪz/　　　2. /s/　/z/　/ɪz/　　　3. /s/　/z/　/ɪz/
4. /s/　/z/　/ɪz/　　　5. /s/　/z/　/ɪz/　　　6. /s/　/z/　/ɪz/

B Listen to the sentences and choose the correct sound.　　1-12

1. /s/　/z/　/ɪz/　　2. /s/　/z/　/ɪz/　　3. /s/　/z/　/ɪz/　　4. /s/　/z/　/ɪz/

C Tongue Twister　　1-13

"The boys and girls took their prizes and gifts on the buses to the schools."

UNIT 1 | *Where shall we go?*

VII Speaking 2

Find out about your classmates. Ask three people the following questions.

	Partner 1	Partner 2	Partner 3
1. Would you like to go on a cruise?			
2. Would you like to go on an adventure vacation?			
3. Would you prefer to travel alone or in a group?			
4. Would you prefer to go diving or skiing on a vacation?			
5. Have you ever been abroad?			
6. What's a country you'd like to visit?			
7. Where would the best place for a honeymoon be?			
8. Your question: _____?			

memo

UNIT 02

Just click there.

Booking a Vacation

I Vocabulary

A Match the English words and phrases (1~10) to the Japanese words (a~j).

1. ____ luxury
2. ____ travel agency
3. ____ accommodations
4. ____ particular
5. ____ budget
6. ____ refundable
7. ____ meal plan
8. ____ direct flight
9. ____ search
10. ____ brochure

| a. 特定の | b. 食事プラン | c. 返金可能 | d. 探す | e. 宿泊施設 |
| f. パンフレット | g. 予算 | h. 豪華な | i. 旅行会社 | j. 直行便 |

B Complete the dialogs with words and phrases from Part A. 1-14~18

1. **A:** What's the longest flight you've ever been on?
   B: It was when I flew from Tokyo to London. It was a(n) _____, but it took 12 hours!

2. **A:** What is your _____ for this vacation?
   B: I can't spend more than ¥100,000, so no luxury hotels this time!

3. **A:** How long do you usually _____ for a vacation before you book one?
   B: Well, I make decisions quickly, so usually about an hour or so. The longest I ever took was two hours, I think.

4. **A:** What's your favorite type of vacation _____?
   B: Hotels. I find them a lot more comfortable than camping in tents or staying in apartments. I can relax more, and I don't need to think about cooking!

5. **A:** What kind of _____ do you usually book?
   B: I like it when breakfast is included, but not lunch or dinner. A good breakfast buffet is great, isn't it?

C Practice the dialogs in Part B with a partner.

D Now, ask your partner the questions in Part B. Give your own responses.

II Listening and Speaking 1   1-19

A Listen to the questions and write them below.

1. _____
2. _____
3. _____
4. _____

B Now, select the best responses from the choices below.

1. **a.** I always do it online.   **b.** JTB is a travel agency.   **c.** It was great.
2. **a.** It was very quick.   **b.** It was a long trip.   **c.** Yes, I do.
3. **a.** No, they're expensive.   **b.** No, I don't think so.   **c.** No, not really.
4. **a.** Yes, it's fun to travel.   **b.** Yes, it looks fun.   **c.** Yes, I like to travel.

C Next, ask your partner the questions in Part A. Give your own responses.

13

III Listening 1-20,21

A Listen to two people talking about booking vacations. Write the places they visited/will visit and check (O) the correct boxes.

1. Place: _____

	Yes	No
• booked online		
• found it easy		
• did it quickly		
• will do it again		

2. Place: _____

	Yes	No
• booked online		
• did it quickly		
• found it easy		
• will do it again		

B Listen to the speakers again. Complete the texts below.

Speaker 1

I booked my vacation last year on the internet. I went to Hokkaido with my friend for a week. We sat (1) _____ in the library at university and used a (2) _____ there. It was really easy and it only took 40 (3) _____. First, we found a hotel we liked, then the (4) _____ gave us a choice of four different flights. We were really happy with our (5) _____ and with the way we booked our vacation. We're going to do it again this year, but we won't go to Hokkaido. Maybe we'll visit Nagano this time.

Speaker 2

I'm not very (1) _____ booking vacations online. I'm worried I'll make a (2) _____ and book the wrong hotel or flight. That's why I always book my trips through a travel agency. I (3) _____ booked a trip to Kyoto. I went to the (4) _____ shop in Shinagawa and got some brochures. I spent some time looking at them that night and went back the next day and (5) _____ to the agent again. It took a while, but it was easy and I'm happy with the booking, so I think I'm going to keep doing it this way.

UNIT 2 | *Just click there.*

IV Speaking 1

Which of the following are important to you when booking a vacation? Check the boxes below and talk to your partner about what they think.

	Very important	Quite important	Not important	Reason
• can see pictures	☐	☐	☐	....
• can read reviews	☐	☐	☐	....
• can do it quickly	☐	☐	☐	....
• can do it easily	☐	☐	☐	....
• there is a lot of choice	☐	☐	☐	....
• _____	☐	☐	☐	....
• _____	☐	☐	☐	....

V Listening and Speaking 2

1-22

A Listen to the conversation and complete the text below.

Ji-ho: How shall we (1)_____ our vacation, online or at a travel agency?

Yoko: Let's do it online. I think it's (2)_____ and **quicker**.

Ji-ho: OK. So, I want a flight and hotel (3)_____. How do I do that?

Yoko: You (4)_____ _____ _____. If you want a particular **type of accommodations**, you can filter choices that way, too.

Ji-ho: Wow! This hotel looks **nice**. It (5)_____ _____ _____ **refundable** as well.

Yoko: So, you've decided already? Booking online is (6)_____ _____ _____ at a travel agency, but not that fast!

B Now, practice the conversation with a partner.

C Next, change the information in *italics* using your own ideas and practice again.

15

VI Pronunciation

《 th の発音：/ð/ /θ/ 》

th の発音には2種類あります。日本語にはない音ですが、舌の位置に注意して練習してみましょう。

1. 有声音の /ð/ は、舌先を歯の間に軽く挟み、音を濁らせて発音します。舌を引きながら発音すると良いでしょう。カタカナのザ、ジ、ゼ、ゾに近い音になります。
   例）there /ð/   than /ð/
2. 無声音の /θ/ も舌先を歯の間に軽く挟みますが、音は濁らず息を吐くように発音します。こちらも舌を引きながら発音します。「スィ」や「スェ」に近い音です。
   例）think /θ/   three /θ/

Exercises

A Listen to the words and choose the correct sound.   1-23

1. /ð/ /θ/   2. /ð/ /θ/   3. /ð/ /θ/
4. /ð/ /θ/   5. /ð/ /θ/   6. /ð/ /θ/

B Listen to the sentences and choose the correct sound.   1-24

1. /ð/ /θ/   2. /ð/ /θ/   3. /ð/ /θ/   4. /ð/ /θ/

C Tongue Twister   1-25

"Think about this thing, that thing, and those things."

VII Speaking 2

Find out about your classmates. Ask three people the following questions.

	Partner 1	Partner 2	Partner 3
1. How do you usually book a vacation?			
2. How long does it take you to book a vacation?			
3. Do you prefer booking vacations online or at a travel agency?			
4. Have you ever made a mistake when booking a vacation?			
5. What's the quickest you've ever booked a vacation?			
6. Do you think booking vacations online is safe?			
7. Which is more important for you when booking a vacation, reviews or photos?			
8. Your question: _____?			

memo

UNIT 03

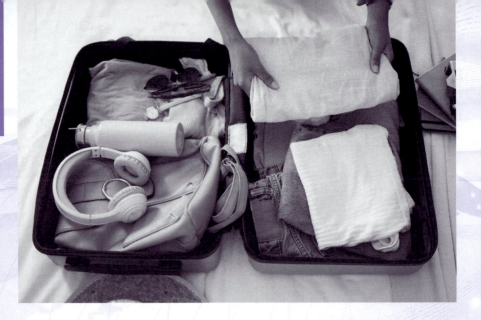

Let's get ready.
Packing and Preparing

I Vocabulary

A Match the English words and phrases (1~10) to the Japanese words (a~j).

1. ____ allowance
2. ____ sunscreen
3. ____ bug bite
4. ____ spare
5. ____ checklist
6. ____ souvenir
7. ____ expensive
8. ____ depends
9. ____ backpack
10. ____ unlimited

a. 土産	b. (〜に) よる	c. 虫刺され	d. 無制限の	e. 日焼け止め剤
f. 許容量	g. 照合表	h. 高価な	i. 予備品	j. リュックサック

B Complete the dialogs with words and phrases from Part A. 1-26~30

1. **A:** How long before you leave on vacation do you usually finish your packing?
   B: Well, that _____ on where I'm going and how long I'm going for.

2. **A:** What is something you always take on vacation?
   B: Definitely some cream or spray for a(n) _____. I really hate feeling itchy, so it's important for me.

3. **A:** How long do you usually spend packing for a vacation?
   B: Not long. I usually make a(n) _____ and that helps.

4. **A:** Have you ever forgotten anything important when packing?
   B: Yes. I usually take a(n) _____ pair of shoes on vacation. I forgot once and it rained so I had to wear wet shoes all weekend.

5. **A:** Do you think _____ suitcases are always better quality?
   B: Not always. I bought a cheap one a few years ago and I still use it now.

C Practice the dialogs in Part B with a partner.

D Now, ask your partner the questions in Part B. Give your own responses.

II Listening and Speaking 1

A Listen to the questions and write them below.

1. _____
2. _____
3. _____
4. _____

B Now, select the best responses from the choices below.

1. **a.** I do my own packing.   **b.** I guess so.   **c.** It took ages!
2. **a.** No, never.   **b.** No, I'm not.   **c.** No, I don't.
3. **a.** Just one.   **b.** They're not mine.   **c.** Are they his?
4. **a.** I can do it.   **b.** Yes, it looks like fun. **c.** Yes, I do.

C Next, ask your partner the questions in Part A. Give your own responses.

III Listening 1-32,33

A Listen to two people talking about preparing for vacations. Write the places they visited and check (O) the correct boxes.

1. Place: _____

	Yes	No
• went for 2 weeks		
• packed early		
• was stressed		
• forgot something		

2. Place: _____

	Yes	No
• went for 2 weeks		
• packed early		
• was stressed		
• forgot something		

B Listen to the speakers again. Complete the texts below.

Speaker 1

(1) _____ say I'm not very organized in general, but when I go on vacation, I like to make sure I've got everything prepared and packed early. Last year, I went (2) _____ in Yamanashi. I only went for two days, but I had everything ready two weeks (3) _____ I left. It might sound crazy, but I feel more relaxed that way. This is especially true when I go on an (4) _____ vacation. I'm really glad that I was so well-prepared because I was sure I had everything I needed, and I had a (5) _____ time.

Speaker 2

In the past, I always left my packing and preparing for a vacation until the last (1) _____. I'd often do it the day before I left or even on the same day. But recently I went on a trip to Canada for a week. I hadn't (2) _____ much at all and just put my (3) _____ clothes in my suitcase. When I got to Canada, it was really cold, and I needed to go to the shops and buy a lot of new (4) _____ clothes. It was a waste of money because I couldn't fit them all in my suitcase on the way back. I won't do that (5) _____ because it was quite stressful.

UNIT 3 | *Let's get ready.*

IV Speaking 1

Which of the following items are important for you to take on a vacation? Check the boxes below and talk to your partner about what they think.

	Very important	Quite important	Not important	Reason
• sunscreen	☐	☐	☐	....
• spare shoes	☐	☐	☐	....
• phone charger	☐	☐	☐	....
• paper map	☐	☐	☐	....
• dictionary	☐	☐	☐	....
• _____	☐	☐	☐	....
• _____	☐	☐	☐	....

V Listening and Speaking 2

1-34

A Listen to the conversation and complete the text below.

Linh: Come on! We're leaving *in two days*. We need to (1) _____ _____ _____.

Suresh: Don't (2) _____. That's lots of time.

Linh: Well, I'd really (3) _____ _____ _____ now. Do you have *the sunscreen*?

Suresh: Yes, I bought it *yesterday*. It's in the (4) _____.

Linh: Good. How (5) _____ *a spare phone charger*?

Suresh: I (6) _____ _____ _____, yet. But I know where it is.

Linh: OK. Do you think we need to take *a dictionary* with us?

Suresh: No, not really. By the way, why am I doing everything? What are you getting ready?

Linh: You!

B Now, practice the conversation with a partner.

C Next, change the information in *italics* using your own ideas and practice again.

21

VI Pronunciation

《 /ɪ/ と /iː/ の発音 》

/ɪ/ と /iː/ の発音は似ているようで異なるため、実際に何度も繰り返して耳と口が慣れるようにしていきましょう。

/ɪ/ の発音：唇を軽く横に広げ、カタカナの「イ」と「エ」の中間くらいの音を短めに発音します。

例）f<u>i</u>nish /ɪ/　　h<u>i</u>story /ɪ/

/iː/ の発音：唇を横に広げ、舌先を上の歯の根元に近づけます。/ɪ/ よりも音を長く発音します。

例）n<u>ee</u>d /iː/　　t<u>ea</u> /iː/

Exercises

A Listen to the words and choose the correct sound. 1-35

1. /ɪ/　/iː/　　2. /ɪ/　/iː/　　3. /ɪ/　/iː/
4. /ɪ/　/iː/　　5. /ɪ/　/iː/　　6. /ɪ/　/iː/

B Listen to the sentences and choose the correct sound. 1-36

1. /ɪ/　/iː/　　2. /ɪ/　/iː/　　3. /ɪ/　/iː/　　4. /ɪ/　/iː/

C Tongue Twister 1-37

"The sheep on the ship felt so seasick."

VII Speaking 2

Find out about your classmates. Ask three people the following questions.

	Partner 1	Partner 2	Partner 3
1. How much luggage would you take on a weekend trip?			
2. How much luggage would you take on a two-week vacation?			
3. Do you prefer backpacks or suitcases?			
4. Have you ever lost a bag or suitcase when traveling?			
5. What are three things that you think people should always take on vacation?			
6. Should baggage allowance on planes be unlimited?			
7. Do you leave space in your luggage for souvenirs when traveling?			
8. Your question: _____?			

memo

UNIT 04

Which gate?
At the Airport (Departing)

I Vocabulary

A Match the English words and phrases (1~10) to the Japanese words (a~j).

1. ____ security
2. ____ terminals
3. ____ scale
4. ____ departure
5. ____ transfer
6. ____ delayed
7. ____ boarding pass
8. ____ aisle seat
9. ____ economy
10. ____ connecting flight

| a. 接続便 | b. 搭乗券 | c. エコノミー | d. 通路側の席 | e. 出発 |
| f. はかり | g. 遅れた | h. 安全 | i. 乗り換え | j. 発着所 |

B Complete the dialogs with words and phrases from Part A. 1-38~42

1. **A:** What's the biggest airport you've ever been to?
   B: I'm not sure. Maybe Narita International Airport. It has three _____.

2. **A:** Which do you prefer, a(n) _____ or a window seat?
   B: Definitely a window seat. I like to look at the scenery below when I'm flying.

24

UNIT 4   *Which gate?*

3. **A:** Have you ever missed a(n) _____?
   B: Yes. Once I was traveling from Chicago to Fukuoka. My first flight took off late, so we couldn't transfer to the next plane in time.

4. **A:** Have you ever had a suitcase that was too heavy, so you needed to pay extra?
   B: Unfortunately, yes. I knew it was going to be too heavy even before I put it on the _____. It was at least 5kg over the limit!

5. **A:** Would you like to fly first class someday?
   B: Of course! It looks so luxurious! But, until I win the lottery, I will need to stay in _____.

C Practice the dialogs in Part B with a partner.

D Now, ask your partner the questions in Part B. Give your own responses.

II Listening and Speaking 1   1-43

A Listen to the questions and write them below.

1. _____
2. _____
3. _____
4. _____

B Now, select the best responses from the choices below.

1. **a.** I always shop online.   **b.** I didn't like shopping.
   c. Yes, the tax-free shops are great.
2. **a.** It was on a tiny island in the Pacific.   **b.** I can't fly.
   c. Yes, I have tried to.
3. **a.** I'm not a pilot.   **b.** No, I often feel sick.   **c.** Yes, I can fly.
4. **a.** Yes, it's fun to travel.   **b.** Yes, that'd be great!   **c.** Yes, I like to travel.

C Next, ask your partner the questions in Part A. Give your own responses.

III Listening 1-44,45

A Listen to two people talking about airports and flights. Write the places they visited and check (O) the correct boxes.

1. Place: _____

	Yes	No
• flew alone		
• was comfortable		
• forgot something		
• flight was delayed		

2. Place: _____

	Yes	No
• flew alone		
• flight was delayed		
• was comfortable		
• forgot something		

B Listen to the speakers again. Complete the texts below.

Speaker 1

A couple of years ago I went to Hawaii on a family vacation. We booked an (1) _____ flight from Haneda because we wanted to sleep on the plane. I requested a window seat because I (2) _____ I wouldn't get disturbed that way. Unfortunately,

the (3) _____ in front of me reclined their seat straight away and didn't move it back until we were landing. The flight was around seven and a half hours long and I couldn't sleep at all because there wasn't enough (4) _____ for me. Next time, I will pay more money and get a seat with (5) _____ leg room.

Speaker 2

Last summer, I flew to Okinawa on a (1) _____ trip. My colleagues had left the day before, so I was by myself. I was actually looking (2) _____ to the flight, but I overslept in the morning and arrived at the airport just 50 minutes before the departure time. I quickly checked-in and rushed to the gate after clearing (3) _____. I was lucky that the plane had been delayed otherwise I may have (4) _____ it. Once I was on the plane, my seat was great, but I had been so worried that I wouldn't be (5) _____ on that I left my bag in the terminal.

26

UNIT 4 | *Which gate?*

IV Speaking 1

Which of the following are important to you when you are at an airport? Check the boxes below and talk to your partner about what they think.

	Very important	Quite important	Not important	Reason
kind staff	☐	☐	☐	
good restaurants	☐	☐	☐	
good shops	☐	☐	☐	
outside viewing area	☐	☐	☐	
big parking lot	☐	☐	☐	
_____	☐	☐	☐	
_____	☐	☐	☐	

V Listening and Speaking 2

1-46

A Listen to the conversation and complete the text below.

Check-in clerk: Good *morning*. May I see your (1) _____ and ticket, please?

Passenger: Yes, of course. Here you are. I'm flying to **San Francisco**.

Check-in clerk: Thank you. Do you have any baggage (2) _____ _____?

Passenger: Yes, *just one suitcase*.

Check-in clerk: OK. Please **put it on** the (3) _____. [After weighing] I'm afraid this is overweight. Your (4) _____ _____ _____ 23kg and **this suitcase is 28kg**.

Passenger: Oh no. So, what can I do?

Check-in clerk: You can either re-pack and move some (5) _____ _____ hand luggage, or you can pay an excess baggage (6) _____.

Passenger: I see. I can't re-pack now, there's no time. Is it OK to pay **by credit card**?

B Now, practice the conversation with a partner.

C Next, change the information in *italics* using your own ideas and practice again.

27

VI Pronunciation

《 /ɔː/ と /ɜː/ の発音 》

/ɔː/ と /ɜː/ は、両方とも音を伸ばして発音します。/ɔː/ は唇を丸め、やや大きくあごを開き、少し強めに音を出します。カタカナの「オー」に近い音です。

例） air**p**ort /ɔː/   l**aw** /ɔː/

/ɜː/ は口の中や舌に力を入れず、少し舌を下げながら喉の奥から音を出します。カタカナの「アー」と「オー」の中間くらいの音です。

例） t**er**minal /ɜː/   l**ear**n /ɜː/

Exercises

A Listen to the words and choose the correct sound.   1-47

1. /ɔː/ /ɜː/   2. /ɔː/ /ɜː/   3. /ɔː/ /ɜː/
4. /ɔː/ /ɜː/   5. /ɔː/ /ɜː/   6. /ɔː/ /ɜː/

B Listen to the sentences and choose the correct sound.   1-48

1. /ɔː/ /ɜː/   2. /ɔː/ /ɜː/   3. /ɔː/ /ɜː/   4. /ɔː/ /ɜː/

C Tongue Twister   1-49

"Four birds on a tour saw thirty thirsty turtles."

UNIT 4 | Which gate?

VII Speaking 2

Find out about your classmates. Ask three people the following questions.

	Partner 1	Partner 2	Partner 3
1. How long before a flight do you like to arrive at an airport?			
2. What is the best airport you have ever been to?			
3. What do you do while you are waiting at an airport?			
4. Have you ever gone to a wrong terminal or gate?			
5. Have you ever had a problem at an airport?			
6. How do you feel during takeoff and landing?			
7. Do you get nervous while clearing security at an airport?			
8. Your question: _____?			

memo

UNIT 05

Where are the taxis?

At the Airport (Arriving)

I Vocabulary

A Match the English words and phrases (1~10) to the Japanese words (a~j).

1. ____ declare
2. ____ customs
3. ____ banned
4. ____ purpose
5. ____ reclaim
6. ____ fares
7. ____ express
8. ____ shuttle bus
9. ____ immigration
10. ____ public transportation

| a. 禁止された | b. 往復バス | c. 急行便 | d. 手荷物受取所 | e. 申告する |
| f. 税関 | g. 目的 | h. 運賃 | i. 入国審査 | j. 公共交通機関 |

B Complete the dialogs with words and phrases from Part A. 1-50~54

1. **A:** Do you like traveling by _____?
   B: Yes. I love trains and buses. I wanted to be a train driver when I was younger.

2. **A:** Do you ever take _____ trains?
   B: Yes. They're so much quicker than local trains that stop at every station.

3. **A:** Are bus _____ in your country expensive?

   B: No, not really. They're quite reasonable actually.

4. **A:** Have you ever gone to a country for a(n) _____ other than a vacation?

   B: Yes. I studied in the Philippines for a month last year.

5. **A:** How do you feel at airport _____?

   B: I'm always a bit nervous. I don't know why. I've never had any problems with my passport or visa.

C Practice the dialogs in Part B with a partner.

D Now, ask your partner the questions in Part B. Give your own responses.

II Listening and Speaking 1   1-55

A Listen to the questions and write them below.

1. _____
2. _____
3. _____
4. _____

B Now, select the best responses from the choices below.

1. **a.** I don't like flying.   **b.** Six times.   **c.** I take the train.
2. **a.** Yes, I have.   **b.** Yes, I was on it.   **c.** It's busy, isn't it?
3. **a.** I like our customs.   **b.** He's not so strict.   **c.** I think so.
4. **a.** About an hour.   **b.** About three bags.   **c.** About 20 meters.

C Next, ask your partner the questions in Part A. Give your own responses.

III Listening  1-56,57

A Listen to two people talking about where they visited/work. Write the places they visited/work and check (O) the correct boxes.

1. Place: _____

	Yes	No
• traveled first class	☐	☐
• landed close to the city	☐	☐
• baggage reclaim was busy	☐	☐
• train journey was bad	☐	☐

2. Place: _____

	Yes	No
• customs is strict	☐	☐
• visitors can get in trouble	☐	☐
• thinks rules are bad	☐	☐
• likes their job	☐	☐

B Listen to the speakers again. Complete the texts below.

Speaker 1

I visited London on vacation a couple of years ago. I booked a (1) _____ flight with a budget airline to save some money, but I didn't realize that meant we would arrive at a small airport that's a long way from the city center. When we (2) _____, it took a long time to get off the plane, even longer to get (3) _____ immigration, and it was really crowded at baggage reclaim when we were (4) _____ our suitcases. Catching the train to the city center wasn't too bad, but I would definitely recommend arriving at a larger and (5) _____ airport.

Speaker 2

I'm a customs (1) _____ at an airport in Sydney. People often say that customs rules in Australia are very strict and they are correct. We have many import conditions on meat, (2) _____, plants, and herbs. Many visitors get into trouble for (3) _____ to bring banned items into the country. This may confuse some tourists, but it is for a good reason as a lot of the prohibited items can cause (4) _____ to the local environment. Sometimes I feel bad for people who get punished, but overall, I think my job is an (5) _____ one that helps my country, so I enjoy it.

UNIT 5 | *Where are the taxis?*

IV Speaking 1

Which of the following are important to you when arriving at an airport? Check the boxes below and talk to your partner about what they think.

	Very important	Quite important	Not important	Reason
• English-speaking staff	☐	☐	☐	
• good signs	☐	☐	☐	
• short lines	☐	☐	☐	
• good transportation links	☐	☐	☐	
• lots of luggage carts	☐	☐	☐	
• _____	☐	☐	☐	
• _____	☐	☐	☐	

V Listening and Speaking 2

1-58

A Listen to the conversation and complete the text below.

Traveler: Hello. I'm staying at **Hotel Paradiso**. Can you (1) _____ me the best way to get there, please?

Information: *Hotel Paradiso*? Sure. The closest station is **Central Station**. Take the **yellow** line for three stops, then (2) _____ to the green line at Bank Street Station.

Traveler: Right. How many stops do I (3) _____ _____ _____ green line for?

Information: From Bank Street Station, it's *just two stops*.

Traveler: (4) _____ _____ _____ I leave **Central Station** from?

Information: Your hotel is *only a 3-minute walk from Exit 2A*.

Traveler: Thank you. Is it easy (5) _____ _____ _____ with luggage?

Information: Oh. I didn't see all of your suitcases. Maybe (6) _____ a taxi would be better.

B Now, practice the conversation with a partner.

C Next, change the information in *italics* using your own ideas and practice again.

VI Pronunciation

《 規則動詞・過去形の発音 》

規則動詞を過去形にするときは、後ろに -d または -ed を付けます。この際、3種類の発音があるので、それらの違いを覚えておきましょう。

/d/ の発音：カタカナの「ドゥ」に近い音になります。動詞の語尾が有声音 [b, v, g, r, z, l, m, n など] で終わる単語で、元の形に d を付けて発音します。

　　　例) arrive<u>d</u> /d/　　declare<u>d</u> /d/

/t/ の発音：唇を尖らせて、カタカナの「トゥ」に近い音を出します。-ed の前が無声子音 [k, f, p, x, s, ʃ, θ など] で終わる場合にこの発言となります。スペルに d が入っていますが、濁らずに発音するので注意しましょう。

　　　例) book<u>ed</u> /t/　　finish<u>ed</u> /t/

/ɪd/ の発音：-ed の直前に d か t がある場合にスペルの前の音と繋げて、カタカナの「ィドゥ」のような発音になります。スペルに e があっても「エ」ではなく小さい「ィ」が入ります。

　　　例) visit<u>ed</u> /ɪd/　　need<u>ed</u> /ɪd/

Exercises

A Listen to the words and choose the correct sound. 1-59

1. /d/　/t/　/ɪd/　　2. /d/　/t/　/ɪd/　　3. /d/　/t/　/ɪd/
4. /d/　/t/　/ɪd/　　5. /d/　/t/　/ɪd/　　6. /d/　/t/　/ɪd/

B Listen to the sentences and choose the correct sound. 1-60

1. /d/　/t/　/ɪd/　　2. /d/　/t/　/ɪd/　　3. /d/　/t/　/ɪd/　　4. /d/　/t/　/ɪd/

C Tongue Twister　　1-61

"They relaxed, laughed, and joked together."
"After they played, they cleaned and dried their shoes."
"They decided they needed more printed books."

VII Speaking 2

Find out about your classmates. Ask three people the following questions.

	Partner 1	Partner 2	Partner 3
1. Do you research an airport before landing there?			
2. Should airports be close to city centers?			
3. Have you ever stayed at a hotel close to an airport?			
4. Is traveling to and from your local airport easy?			
5. Would you like to be an immigration or customs officer?			
6. Would you prefer to travel from an airport by taxi or public transport?			
7. Have you ever had a problem when arriving at an airport?			
8. Your question: _____?			

memo

UNIT 06

Welcome!

Checking In

I Vocabulary

A Match the English words and phrases (1~10) to the Japanese words (a~j).

1. ____ receptionist
2. ____ front desk
3. ____ lobby
4. ____ share
5. ____ attended
6. ____ floor
7. ____ reservation
8. ____ luggage
9. ____ policy
10. ____ arrive

a. 方針	**b.** 階	**c.** 予約	**d.** 受付係	**e.** 到着する
f. 荷物	**g.** フロントデスク	**h.** 参加した	**i.** ロビー	**j.** 共有する

B Complete the dialogs with words and phrases from Part A. 1-62~66

1. **A:** Do you think it is important for a hotel to have a nice lobby?
   B: Yes, I do. The lobby is where the _____ is, so you will probably go there a lot during your stay. It also gives you a good idea of the style and quality of the hotel.

2. **A:** Have you ever _____ a wedding in a hotel?
   B: No, I haven't. But I did go to a conference in Prague last year. It was held in a big hotel in the center of the city.

36

3. **A:** Do you prefer smoking or non-smoking rooms?
   B: Non-smoking rooms. I had to _____ a hotel room with a smoker once and I had a sore throat the whole time we were there.

4. **A:** What should I do if I lose my room key?
   B: Please tell the _____ as quickly as possible and they will issue you with a new one.

5. **A:** Do you have a credit card?
   B: Yes, I do. But I would prefer to pay for my room in cash. Is that okay?
   A: Yes, you can pay for your room in cash. But I still need to scan your credit card. I'm sorry, but it is hotel _____.

C Practice the dialogs in Part B with a partner.

D Now, ask your partner the questions in Part B. Give your own responses.

II Listening and Speaking 1

A Listen to the questions and write them below.

1. _____
2. _____
3. _____
4. _____

B Now, select the best responses from the choices below.

1. a. Yes, I have.   b. Three times.   c. No, not yet.
2. a. Yes, it's great. b. No, I can't see it. c. Yes, it is.
3. a. The third.   b. The last.   c. It's in the lobby.
4. a. Not yet.   b. Never.   c. Definitely not.

C Next, ask your partner the questions in Part A. Give your own responses.

III Listening 1-68,69

A Listen to two people talking about checking in at hotels. Write the places they visited/work and check (O) the correct boxes.

1. Place: _____

	Yes	No
• works in a hotel	☐	☐
• lives abroad	☐	☐
• booked a room	☐	☐
• went to the wrong hotel	☐	☐

2. Place: _____

	Yes	No
• works in a hotel	☐	☐
• got married	☐	☐
• lives abroad	☐	☐
• went to the wrong hotel	☐	☐

B Listen to the speakers again. Complete the texts below.

Speaker 1

Hi, I'm Eriko and I'm from Japan. I work on the front desk of a (1) _____ hotel in Port Louis in Mauritius. I'm usually the first (2) _____ of the hotel staff that a guest meets, so it's really important to make a good first (3) _____. After making sure that the guest has a reservation and that they are in the correct hotel, I check how long they will stay and that they have (4) _____ the right kind of room. Putting a guest in the wrong kind of room can make them unhappy and ruin their stay. They may even (5) _____ about the hotel.

Speaker 2

I went to Phnom Penh in Cambodia last year to (1) _____ my friend's wedding. It was the first time I'd left my country, and I had a fantastic time. But I also had a lot of (2) _____ checking in to the hotel. When I arrived at the hotel, I told the receptionist my name and that I had booked a room. But when he checked the hotel computer, he couldn't find my (3) _____. When I showed him the email (4) _____ my booking, he started laughing. I was in the Palace Gate Hotel. I had booked a room in the Anik Palace Hotel, which was one block away. I was so (5) _____!

38

UNIT 6 | Welcome!

IV Speaking 1

Which of the following are important to you when checking in to a hotel? Check the boxes below and talk to your partner about what they think.

	Very important	Quite important	Not important	Reason
• speed of check-in	☐	☐	☐	
• polite staff	☐	☐	☐	
• check-in time	☐	☐	☐	
• luggage storage	☐	☐	☐	
• porters	☐	☐	☐	
• _____	☐	☐	☐	
• _____	☐	☐	☐	

V Listening and Speaking 2

1-70

A Listen to the conversation and complete the text below.

Receptionist: Welcome to Hotel Paradiso! How (1) _____ I help you?

Guest: Hello. I'd like to check in. I **have a reservation in the name of** Oliveira.

Receptionist: Certainly, Ms. Oliveira. Just let me check. Ah, here it is. You will be (2) _____ _____ _____ until **the 25th of June**?

Guest: Yes, that's right. I'm here for a **conference** (3) _____ week.

Receptionist: Oh, that's (4) _____ . May I scan your credit card, Ms. Oliveira?

Guest: Sure. Here you are.

Receptionist: Thank you. You **are in room 1804**. I'll (5) _____ _____ _____ key. While I do that, can I ask you to **fill out** this registration card?

Guest: No problem. (6) _____ _____ _____ , can you tell me **where the Business Center is**?

B Now, practice the conversation with a partner.

C Next, change the information in *italics* using your own ideas and practice again.

39

VI Pronunciation

【LとRの発音：/l/ /r/】

日本人にとって難しい発音に、LとRの違いがあります。カタカナのラリルレロで覚えてしまうと、区別できなくなるので注意しましょう。

　Lの発音：舌を上向きにして、上の歯の根元に付けるように発音します。
　　　　例）l̲obby　/l/　　fl̲y　/l/
　Rの発音：口の中のどこにも舌先を付けずに、口の奥の方で発音します。
　　　　例）r̲oom　/r/　　r̲oad　/r/

Exercises

A Listen to the words and choose the correct sound.　　1-71

1. /l/ /r/　　　2. /l/ /r/　　　3. /l/ /r/
4. /l/ /r/　　　5. /l/ /r/　　　6. /l/ /r/

B Listen to the sentences and choose the correct sound.　　1-72

1. /l/ /r/　　2. /l/ /r/　　3. /l/ /r/　　4. /l/ /r/

C Tongue Twister　　1-73

"Red lorry, yellow lorry, green lorry, yellow lorry."

VII Speaking 2

Find out about your classmates. Ask three people the following questions.

	Partner 1	Partner 2	Partner 3
1. Have you ever stayed in a hotel?			
2. Was it easy to check in?			
3. How long did it take?			
4. Were the receptionists polite?			
5. What language did you use to check in?			
6. What was the hotel lobby like?			
7. Would you like to stay in that hotel again?			
8. Your question: _____?			

memo

UNIT 07

This isn't right.
Resolving Problems

I Vocabulary

A Match the English words and phrases (1~10) to the Japanese words (a~j).

1. ____ available
2. ____ complaint
3. ____ stain
4. ____ noisy
5. ____ resolve
6. ____ humid
7. ____ book
8. ____ strange
9. ____ crack
10. ____ amenities

a. 予約する	b. 苦情	c. うるさい	d. ひび、割れ目	e. 染み
f. 解決する	g. アメニティ	h. 奇妙な、不思議な	i. 利用できる	j. 湿気の多い

B Complete the dialogs with words and phrases from Part A.   1-74~78

1. **A:** Have you ever had a problem when you stayed in a hotel?
   B: Yes. Once I booked a room at a hotel, but when I arrived, they didn't have a reservation in my name. Luckily, they had a room _____ so I could stay there, but I was a bit shocked at first.

2. **A:** What would you do if your hotel room had a(n) _____ smell?
   B: I'd call reception right away and ask to be moved.

42

3. **A:** Have you ever made a(n) _____ at a hotel before?
   B: Yes. There was a crack in the bathroom mirror, and I thought it was dangerous. The hotel staff were really helpful.

4. **A:** Have you ever stayed in a(n) _____ hotel?
   B: Yes. In one room I stayed in the air conditioner didn't work well and it was really loud.

5. **A:** What is the worst hotel you've ever stayed in?
   B: Three years ago, I went to a hotel and the room they gave me had a blood _____ on the wall. I left very quickly and moved to a hotel I felt safer in!

C Practice the dialogs in Part B with a partner.

D Now, ask your partner the questions in Part B. Give your own responses.

II Listening and Speaking 1   1-79

A Listen to the questions and write them below.

1. _____
2. _____
3. _____
4. _____

B Now, select the best responses from the choices below.

1. a. It was a great vacation.   b. I lost my wallet once.
   c. The guests had a problem.

2. a. No, it was in the city.   b. Yes! It had a jungle theme.
   c. Why was it strange?

3. a. Definitely air conditioning. b. I couldn't find the hair dryer.
   c. There were only three hangers.

4. a. Yes, they were noisy.   b. Families can be noisy.
   c. It depends on how noisy they were.

C Next, ask your partner the questions in Part A. Give your own responses.

III Listening

 1-80,81

A Listen to two people talking about vacation problems. Write the problems they had and check (O) the correct boxes.

1. Problem: _____

	Yes	No
• traveled alone	☐	☐
• problem was in their room	☐	☐
• asked for help	☐	☐
• problem was resolved	☐	☐

2. Problem: _____

	Yes	No
• traveled alone	☐	☐
• problem was in their room	☐	☐
• asked for help	☐	☐
• problem was resolved	☐	☐

B Listen to the speakers again. Complete the texts below.

Speaker 1

I went on a trip with a friend from my rugby club a couple of years ago. We were really looking forward to going, but we had a problem. We had booked a (1) _____ room, a room with two single beds. But when we (2) _____, we found that the hotel had put us in a room with one (3) _____ bed. We asked to move rooms, but none were (4) _____ so we had to share a bed for the night. It was really awkward and (5) _____.

Speaker 2

Two years ago, I really needed a (1) _____, restful vacation. So, I booked a room for myself in a hotel that looked really nice. When I got there, it was great, but my (2) _____ started at night. The people in the room next to me were (3) _____ very noisy and shouting a lot. I couldn't rest or sleep at all. I called (4) _____ and complained. They came to our floor and asked the other guests to be (5) _____ and it worked. I slept really well after that.

44

UNIT 7 | *This isn't right.*

IV Speaking 1

Which of the following would be serious problems for you in a hotel? Check the boxes below and talk to your partner about what they think.

	Very serious	Quite serious	Not serious	Reason
• dirty room	☐	☐	☐	
• noisy guests	☐	☐	☐	
• closed facilities	☐	☐	☐	
• broken amenities	☐	☐	☐	
• unhelpful staff	☐	☐	☐	
• _____	☐	☐	☐	
• _____	☐	☐	☐	

V Listening and Speaking 2

1-82

A Listen to the conversation and complete the text below.

Receptionist: Good evening, this is reception.

Guest: Good evening. I'm in room *621*. I can't (1) _____ the **remote control for the air conditioner**.

Receptionist: Room *621*? It (2) _____ be **on the wall next to the door**.

Guest: No, I (3) _____ there already. It isn't there.

Receptionist: I'm very (4) _____ _____ _____. I will send someone up right away with a spare **remote**.

Guest: Yes, please do. (5) _____ _____ _____.

Receptionist: Is (6) _____ _____ _____ I can help you with?

Guest: No, thank you. That's it.

B Now, practice the conversation with a partner.

C Next, change the information in *italics* using your own ideas and practice again.

45

VI Pronunciation

【s と sh の発音：/s/ /ʃ/】

単語のスペルにある s の発音記号は /s/ と表現され、日本語の「サ・シ・ス・セ・ソ」と近い音になります。口を横に広げるイメージで発音してみましょう。

　　例）s<u>i</u>ngle /s/　　s<u>i</u>t /s/

また、sh の発音記号は /ʃ/ と表現され、日本語の「シュ」と「シ」の間くらいの音になります。唇を少し前に出すイメージで発音してみましょう。

　　例）<u>sh</u>outing /ʃ/　　<u>sh</u>ine /ʃ/

Exercises

A Listen to the words and choose the correct sound. 1-83

1. /s/　/ʃ/　　2. /s/　/ʃ/　　3. /s/　/ʃ/
4. /s/　/ʃ/　　5. /s/　/ʃ/　　6. /s/　/ʃ/

B Listen to the sentences and choose the correct sound. 1-84

1. /s/　/ʃ/　　2. /s/　/ʃ/　　3. /s/　/ʃ/　　4. /s/　/ʃ/

C Tongue Twister 1-85

　　"She sells seashells on the seashore."

UNIT 7 | *This isn't right.*

VII Speaking 2

Find out about your classmates. Ask three people the following questions.

	Partner 1	Partner 2	Partner 3
1. Have you ever had a problem on a vacation?			
2. Have you ever made a complaint in a hotel?			
3. What is the worst problem a hotel can have?			
4. Are you good at resolving problems?			
5. Are hotel staff in your country generally helpful?			
6. What would you do if your hotel room was dirty?			
7. Do customers in your country often complain?			
8. Your question: _____?			

memo

UNIT 08

Let's work out.

Hotel Facilities and Services

I Vocabulary

A Match the English words and phrases (1~10) to the Japanese words (a~j).

1. ____ sauna
2. ____ massage
3. ____ rest
4. ____ complimentary
5. ____ seasonal
6. ____ prefer
7. ____ opposite
8. ____ laundry
9. ____ conference
10. ____ specialist

a. 無料の	b. マッサージ	c. 洗濯	d. 専門家	e. 休む
f. 向かい側の	g. 会議	h. 季節の	i. サウナ	j. ～の方を好む

B Complete the dialogs with words and phrases from Part A.   1-86~90

1. **A:** Do you like staying in hotels?
   B: Yes, I do. Especially if they have a(n) _____ or fitness center. I like to go there and sweat out my problems.

2. **A:** Do you often use swimming pools in hotels?
   B: Yes, but unfortunately, the last hotel I stayed in only had a(n) _____ pool, so it was closed when I went in December.

48

UNIT 8 | Let's work out.

3. **A:** Which do you _____ when you stay in a hotel, getting room service or going out to eat?
   B: Definitely going out to eat. I think just staying in a hotel room is boring.

4. **A:** Have you ever had a(n) _____ at a hotel?
   B: No, I always worry about how good it will be. I'd rather go to a specialist.

5. **A:** How important to you is it for a hotel to have a coin _____ service?
   B: Not at all. When I go on vacation I want to relax, not wash my clothes!

C Practice the dialogs in Part B with a partner.

D Now, ask your partner the questions in Part B. Give your own responses.

II Listening and Speaking 1

1-91

A Listen to the questions and write them below.

1. _____
2. _____
3. _____
4. _____

B Now, select the best responses from the choices below.

1. **a.** No, I couldn't.   **b.** No, not really.   **c.** I'm not sure.
2. **a.** Definitely room service.   **b.** There aren't many services.   **c.** The facilities.
3. **a.** No, I don't like exercising. **b.** The hotel does have one.   **c.** I'm not very fit.
4. **a.** Is there one?   **b.** It's expensive.   **c.** It depends.

C Next, ask your partner the questions in Part A. Give your own responses.

49

III Listening 1-92,93

A Listen to two people talking about hotel facilities or services they have used. Write the facilities or services they used and check (O) the correct boxes.

1. Facility / Service: _____

	Yes	No
• was in the hotel		
• was free		
• was good quality		
• was surprised		

2. Facility / Service: _____

	Yes	No
• was in the hotel		
• was free		
• was good quality		
• was surprised		

B Listen to the speakers again. Complete the texts below.

Speaker 1

The last time I (1) _____ in a hotel, I was both lucky and unlucky. It rained all of the time we were there, so we (2) _____ go out. But it was fun using room service. We ordered lots of food and drinks to our room and just (3) _____ there. It was quite expensive, but the quality was good. The (4) _____ member who brought us our meals wanted a tip every time, so I was shocked and (5) _____. That doesn't happen in Japan.

Speaker 2

When I last stayed at a hotel, I used the (1) _____ pool every day. It was quite inconvenient (2) _____ it was in the building opposite the hotel. But it was cheap, and it wasn't far to (3) _____, so it was okay. It was a little bit small, and it wasn't great quality, but it looked clean, so it was fine for me. Actually, I was surprised that it was so (4) _____, I thought there would be more people in there but I (5) _____ saw anyone else there.

UNIT 8 | *Let's work out.*

IV Speaking 1

What kind of hotel facilities and services are important to you? Check the boxes below and talk to your partner about what they think.

	Very important	Quite important	Not important	Reason
• free parking	☐	☐	☐	....
• swimming pool	☐	☐	☐	....
• spa / onsen	☐	☐	☐	....
• restaurant	☐	☐	☐	....
• room service	☐	☐	☐	....
• _____	☐	☐	☐	....
• _____	☐	☐	☐	....

V Listening and Speaking 2

1-94

A Listen to the conversation and complete the text below.

Emma: Now we've had a bit of time to (1) _____, what do you want to do?

Keito: I'm not (2) _____. There's lots to do here. Do you want to go to the *fitness center*?

Emma: No, not yet. *I'm too tired*. What (3) _____ is there?

Keito: We could go to the *sauna*. I haven't been in (4) _____ _____ _____ for a very long time.

Emma: Now that (5) _____ _____ _____. Shall we really treat ourselves and *get a massage*, too?

Keito: Yes! (6) _____ _____ _____ order room *service*. That would be perfect!

B Now, practice the conversation with a partner.

C Next, change the information in *italics* using your own ideas and practice again.

51

VI Pronunciation

【 t と ch の発音：/t/ /tʃ/ 】

英語には発音によって意味が異なってしまうものがあります。/t/ と /tʃ/ の発音もその一つです。アルファベットの t の発音 /t/ は舌先を上の歯と歯茎の境目にあてはじくように音を出します。例）　tip /t/　　art /t/

英語の ch の綴りには３通りの発音がありますが、ここでは /tʃ/ の発音を練習します。唇を丸くして少し尖らせるようにして、息をやや強めに出して発音します。カタカナのチ、チャ、チェに近い音です。　例）　cheap /tʃ/　　arch /tʃ/

Exercises

A Listen to the words and choose the correct sound.   1-95

1. /t/ /tʃ/   2. /t/ /tʃ/   3. /t/ /tʃ/
4. /t/ /tʃ/   5. /t/ /tʃ/   6. /t/ /tʃ/

B Listen to the sentences and choose the correct sound.   1-96

1. /t/ /tʃ/   2. /t/ /tʃ/   3. /t/ /tʃ/   4. /t/ /tʃ/

C Tongue Twister   1-97

"The charity took twenty-two chairs to church."

UNIT 8 | *Let's work out.*

VII Speaking 2

Find out about your classmates. Ask three people the following questions.

	Partner 1	Partner 2	Partner 3
1. What is your favorite hotel facility?			
2. How important are hotel facilities to you?			
3. Which is more important to you, the hotel location or hotel facilities?			
4. Have you ever stayed somewhere because it had good facilities?			
5. Do you think all hotel facilities should be free for hotel guests?			
6. Do you like looking around hotel gift shops?			
7. Do you ever use hotel facilities when you're not a guest?			
8. Your question: _____?			

memo

UNIT 09

Where's the station?

Getting Around Town

I Vocabulary

A Match the English words and phrases (1~10) to the Japanese words (a~j).

1. _____ go straight
2. _____ turn
3. _____ follow
4. _____ next to
5. _____ directions
6. _____ behind
7. _____ traffic lights
8. _____ near
9. _____ explore
10. _____ across from

| a. 行き方 | b. 信号機 | c. 調査する | d. 〜の近くに | e. 曲がる |
| f. 〜の向かいに | g. 沿って進む | h. 後に | i. 〜の隣に | j. まっすぐ行く |

B Complete the dialogs with words and phrases from Part A. 2-01~05

1. **A:** Excuse me. Do you know where the supermarket is?
   B: Sure. _____ down this road and it's on the left. You can't miss it.

2. **A:** How do I get to the station from here?
   B: _____ this road to the town center. The station is between the supermarket and the police station.

UNIT 9 **Where's the station?**

3. **A:** Can you tell me where the nearest convenience store is, please?
   B: No worries. When you leave this building, _____ right and walk for two blocks. It's on the right, next to the library.

4. **A:** Can you tell me the way to the library, please?
   B: From here, take the first right, then the second left. It's on the left, just past the _____. Why don't I show you the way?
   A: That would be great. Thank you.

5. **A:** Could you tell me if there is a coffee shop _____ here, please?
   B: Yes, there's one in this building on the fifth floor. If you take this elevator, the coffee shop will be opposite you when you get off.

C Practice the dialogs in Part B with a partner.

D Now, ask your partner the questions in Part B. Give your own responses.

II Listening and Speaking 1   2-06

A Listen to the questions and write them below.

1. _____
2. _____
3. _____
4. _____

B Now, select the best responses from the choices below.

1. **a.** Yes, I do.   **b.** Yes, three times.   **c.** Yes, I have.
2. **a.** Yes, always.   **b.** Yes, it often does.   **c.** Yes, on my phone.
3. **a.** No, not really.   **b.** Yes, I got it.   **c.** Not very often.
4. **a.** Yes, I could.   **b.** Yes, I can.   **c.** Yes, I did.

C Next, ask your partner the questions in Part A. Give your own responses.

III Listening 2-07,08

A Listen to two people talking about tours and trips. Write the places they visited/will visit and check (O) the correct boxes.

1. Place: _____

	Yes	No
• went with friends	☐	☐
• got lost	☐	☐
• likes tea	☐	☐
• took a tour	☐	☐

2. Place: _____

	Yes	No
• works in a hotel	☐	☐
• cooks food	☐	☐
• took a tour	☐	☐
• lives abroad	☐	☐

B Listen to the speakers again. Complete the texts below.

Speaker 1

Last year, I traveled to Beijing in China for a vacation. It was the first time I had been (1) _____ by myself, so I was excited and a little nervous. On the first day, I wanted to go sightseeing, so I asked the hotel receptionist for (2) _____ to Tiananmen Square. She told me to go straight and then take the first right. But I took a wrong turn and (3) _____ left instead of right. I did find a small square, but it was (4) _____ not Tiananmen Square, which is huge. There was a nice tea shop there, though. The next day, I took a (5) _____ from the hotel.

Speaker 2

I work as a tour (1) _____ in Naples in Italy. People have been living here for nearly three (2) _____ years, so there are lots of historical places to visit. My favorite tour is one which (3) _____ Neapolitan food. First, we take Line 2 for three stops and have breakfast in the Piazza del Plebiscito. Then, we go all the way to Quarto di Marano and catch a ferry to Capri Island for lunch. It's known for having the best pasta and seafood in Italy. Finally, we take Line 2 to the end of the line at Villa Literno and have (4) _____ Neapolitan pizza for dinner. Pizza was (5) _____ in Naples. I love helping my guests experience real Italian food in my hometown.

UNIT 9 | Where's the station?

IV Speaking 1

Which of the following are important to you when traveling around? Check the boxes below and talk to your partner about what they think.

	Very important	Quite important	Not important	Reason
• easy to read signs	☐	☐	☐	....
• friendly tour guides	☐	☐	☐	....
• navigation apps	☐	☐	☐	....
• good quality maps	☐	☐	☐	....
• good guidebooks	☐	☐	☐	....
• _____	☐	☐	☐	....
• _____	☐	☐	☐	....

V Listening and Speaking 2

2-09

A Listen to the conversation and complete the text below.

Tour guide: Welcome to *the London Bus Tour*. I'm Mark, your guide. First, we will (1) _____ _____ _____ *Oxford Street, which is the busiest shopping street in Europe*.

Traveler: Will we have time to go shopping?

Tour guide: We will when we come back. Now, we will (2) _____ left *into Regent Street. Its beautiful buildings were designed by John Nash and James Burton*.

Traveler: Can we stop to take some pictures?

Tour guide: Yes, in just a (3) _____. Now we have (4) _____ in *Piccadilly Square. The Shaftesbury Memorial is* (5) _____ _____ _____. *It is a statue of the Greek god Anteros*. We will stop here for 15 (6) _____ _____ _____ to the next stop.

Traveler: Okay, everyone, let's get a picture *in front of the statue*.

B Now, practice the conversation with a partner.

C Next, change the information in *italics* using your own ideas and practice again.

57

VI Pronunciation

【/r/ と /w/ の発音】

/r/ と /w/ の発音の違いは意外とわかりにくいので、ポイントを押さえておきましょう。

　/r/ の発音：唇を少しすぼめて口の中のどこにも舌先を付けずに、口の奥の方で発音します。

　　　　例）right /r/　　ring /r/

　/w/ の発音：唇を r の時よりもさらにすぼめ、発音しながら口を開くイメージです。口の前の方で発音します。

　　　　例）way /w/　　wing /w/

Exercises

A Listen to the words and choose the correct sound.

1. /r/ /w/　　　2. /r/ /w/　　　3. /r/ /w/
4. /r/ /w/　　　5. /r/ /w/　　　6. /r/ /w/

B Listen to the sentences and choose the correct sound.

1. /r/ /w/　　2. /r/ /w/　　3. /r/ /w/　　4. /r/ /w/

C Tongue Twister

"The woman wearing red ran well and won the wonderful race."

VII Speaking 2

Find out about your classmates. Ask three people the following questions.

	Partner 1	Partner 2	Partner 3
1. Have you ever given someone directions?			
2. Have you ever asked for directions?			
3. Have you ever taken a wrong turn?			
4. Is it easy to get around your hometown?			
5. Can you find new places easily?			
6. Do you prefer to take a tour or find places yourself?			
7. Do you buy a guidebook when you travel?			
8. Your question: _____?			

memo

UNIT 10

Look at that!

Sights and Tourist Spots

I Vocabulary

A Match the English words and phrases (1~10) to the Japanese words (a~j).

1. ____ popular
2. ____ museum
3. ____ recommend
4. ____ impressive
5. ____ in advance
6. ____ landmark
7. ____ admission fee
8. ____ crowded
9. ____ capacity
10. ____ statue

| a. 前もって | b. 博物館 | c. 収容能力 | d. 混み合った | e. 薦める |
| f. 彫像 | g. 歴史的建造物 | h. 人気のある | i. 入場料 | j. 印象的な |

B Complete the dialogs with words and phrases from Part A. 2-13~17

1. **A:** Where would you _____ someone visiting your country go?
   B: I think tourists should definitely visit the Golden Temple in Kyoto. It is very impressive.

2. **A:** What is the most popular place to visit in your hometown?
   B: It's probably the soccer stadium. It has a(n) _____ of 80,000 people, and the tours around it are very good, too.

UNIT 10 **Look at that!**

3. **A:** Is there a good museum near here?
   B: Yes, the national museum is excellent. But if you want to go there, make sure you buy a ticket _____. It often gets very busy.

4. **A:** I want to go somewhere quiet. Do you have any ideas?
   B: Sure. You should go for a walk along the river. It's really beautiful and it never gets _____ there.

5. **A:** Do you like visiting art galleries?
   B: Yes. In my hometown there are many great art galleries that I love. The best thing is that some of them don't charge a(n) _____.

C Practice the dialogs in Part B with a partner.

D Now, ask your partner the questions in Part B. Give your own responses.

II Listening and Speaking 1   2-18

A Listen to the questions and write them below.

1. _____
2. _____
3. _____
4. _____

B Now, select the best responses from the choices below.

1. **a.** The guide was great.   **b.** It was in Rome.   **c.** I prefer going to the beach.
2. **a.** No, it wasn't free.   **b.** Yes, it's so easy.   **c.** Yes, that would be better.
3. **a.** Definitely Landmark Tower. **b.** Not my hometown.   **c.** I haven't been there.
4. **a.** No, not yet.   **b.** Not at all.   **c.** No-one has.

C Next, ask your partner the questions in Part A. Give your own responses.

III Listening

A Listen to two people talking about sights and tourist spots. Write the places they talk about and check (O) the correct boxes.

1. Place: _____

	Yes	No
• is in speaker's hometown	☐	☐
• is internationally famous	☐	☐
• would recommend	☐	☐
• can enter it	☐	☐

2. Place: _____

	Yes	No
• is in speaker's hometown	☐	☐
• is internationally famous	☐	☐
• is noisy	☐	☐
• would recommend	☐	☐

B Listen to the speakers again. Complete the texts below.

Speaker 1

I'm going to tell you about one of the most famous landmarks, not only in my city, but in the (1)_____! It's 93 meters tall and it was (2)_____ to the public in 1886. Nowadays, over 3 million people visit this landmark every year and I think everyone should go there. If you want to go to the top, you can get an elevator part of the way, but after that you have to (3)_____ up some steps. It takes about 20 minutes to get to the top. The landmark was paid for by the people of France and it was gifted to the people of my country as a symbol of (4)_____ and freedom. It is a statue of a lady (5)_____ a torch and a tablet. Do you know what the landmark is? It's the Statue of Liberty!

Speaker 2

The most interesting sightseeing tour I've ever been on was a walking tour around Marrakech I went on when I was on vacation in Morrocco. We (1)_____ Koutoubia Mosque, Bahia Palace, and then walked through some of the souks in Medina. Souks are (2)_____ and the ones in Medina are famous all over the world. They were noisy, (3)_____, and full of energy. It felt strange and scary at first, but I soon realized that I'd be safe if I was (4)_____ and respectful. If you ever visit this part of the world, you should definitely go to a souk. I bought a beautiful cashmere scarf, and the food was (5)_____, too.

UNIT 10 **Look at that!**

IV Speaking 1

Which of the following are important to you when planning where to visit and go sightseeing? Check the boxes below and talk to your partner about what they think.

	Very important	Quite important	Not important	Reason
• is crowded	☐	☐	☐	
• admission fees	☐	☐	☐	
• transport / access	☐	☐	☐	
• has tour guides	☐	☐	☐	
• is famous	☐	☐	☐	
• _____	☐	☐	☐	
• _____	☐	☐	☐	

V Listening and Speaking 2

2-21

A Listen to the conversation and complete the text below.

Traveler: Hello. I'd like to go on a sightseeing tour (1)_____ the city *tomorrow*.

Booking agent: I see. Would you like a full-day or a half-day (2)_____?

Traveler: What does the full-day tour (3)_____?

Booking agent: It's *a six-hour* tour that covers the (4)_____ _____ _____ like *the national gallery, the history museum*, and there's also a river cruise.

Traveler: (5)_____ _____ _____. When and where does it start?

Booking agent: (6)_____ _____ _____ outside *this office* at 10 a.m. The price is *$120* for adults and *$80* for children.

B Now, practice the conversation with a partner.

C Next, change the information in *italics* using your own ideas and practice again.

VI Pronunciation

《 /f/ と /v/ の発音 》

どちらも日本語にない音ですが、練習して発音に慣れるようにしましょう。

/f/ の発音：上の前歯を下唇に軽くあて、隙間から空気を出すように発音します。カタカナの「フ」とは異なるので、注意しましょう。

例) famous /f/　friend /f/

/v/ の発音：/f/ と同じく、上の前歯を下唇に軽くあて、隙間から空気を出すようにしますが、こちらは声帯を震わせて声を出します。

例) vacation /v/　travel /v/

Exercises

A Listen to the words and choose the correct sound. 2-22

1. /f/　/v/
2. /f/　/v/
3. /f/　/v/
4. /f/　/v/
5. /f/　/v/
6. /f/　/v/

B Listen to the sentences and choose the correct sound. 2-23

1. /f/　/v/
2. /f/　/v/
3. /f/　/v/
4. /f/　/v/

C Tongue Twister 2-24

"I felt very funny after a flight from Venice on Friday evening."

VII Speaking 2

Find out about your classmates. Ask three people the following questions.

	Partner 1	Partner 2	Partner 3
1. Have you ever been on a sightseeing tour?			
2. Where would you like to go sightseeing?			
3. Have you ever visited the same sight or tourist spot more than once?			
4. What's the best sight or tourist spot you've ever been to?			
5. Would you prefer to visit a museum or go on a bus tour?			
6. Is there a landmark symbol of your hometown?			
7. Is there a landmark symbol of your country?			
8. Your question: _____?			

memo

UNIT 11

Why are they doing that?

Local Culture

I Vocabulary

A Match the English words and phrases (1~10) to the Japanese words (a~j).

1. ____ traditional
2. ____ ceremony
3. ____ invite
4. ____ festival
5. ____ take part in
6. ____ experience
7. ____ preserve
8. ____ custom
9. ____ event
10. ____ religious

- a. 祭
- b. 式典
- c. 保存する
- d. 習慣・風習
- e. 伝統的な
- f. 行事・催し
- g. 宗教的な
- h. 招待する
- i. 体験
- j. 参加する

B Complete the dialogs with words and phrases from Part A.   2-25~29

1. **A:** Do you ever take part in your local festival?
   B: Yes, I do. Our way of life is changing very quickly, so I think it is important for us to _____ our culture and remember how we used to live.

2. **A:** What's a famous _____ in your country?
   B: I think everyone knows that in Japan we take our shoes off when we enter someone's home. But I think that maybe people do the same thing in lots of other countries, too.

66

3. **A:** Is there a cultural _____ that you recommend?
   B: You've come at the right time. The biggest firework festival of the year takes place in two days. It's world famous. Would you like to book a ticket?

4. **A:** Can you tell me about the traditional wedding _____ in your country?
   B: Well, maybe the most important part is that the people getting married exchange wedding rings and make special promises called oaths to each other.

5. **A:** Have you ever been to a big music festival?
   B: Yes, I've been to the Fuji Rock festival. I had a(n) _____ I'll never forget.

C Practice the dialogs in Part B with a partner.

D Now, ask your partner the questions in Part B. Give your own responses.

II Listening and Speaking 1

A Listen to the questions and write them below.
1. _____
2. _____
3. _____
4. _____

B Now, select the best responses from the choices below.

1. **a.** Yes, they're beautiful.   **b.** No, I didn't.   **c.** Yes, I can see them.
2. **a.** Yes, I go every year.   **b.** I'll go next year.   **c.** Maybe I can go next year.
3. **a.** No, it's a spring event.   **b.** Yes, in the winter.   **c.** Definitely summer events.
4. **a.** Yes, I can dance.   **b.** Yes, I know some.   **c.** No, we're not dancing.

C Next, ask your partner the questions in Part A. Give your own responses.

III Listening 2-31,32

A Listen to two people talking about their experiences of foreign cultures. Write the events they talk about and check (O) the correct boxes.

1. Event: _____

	Yes	No
• is from Mongolia	☐	☐
• went to a festival	☐	☐
• swam in a lake	☐	☐
• tried wrestling	☐	☐

2. Event: _____

	Yes	No
• works in a hotel	☐	☐
• got married	☐	☐
• painted his hands	☐	☐
• ate an egg	☐	☐

B Listen to the speakers again. Complete the texts below.

Speaker 1

I worked in Mongolia for a few years. It's a beautiful (1) _____, but the winters are really cold. Sometimes it gets as cold as –40°C. I was living near Lake Khövsgöl, and I was really surprised that the (2) _____ lake, which is 136km long, turned to ice in the winter. I was even more surprised that the local people have a big (3) _____ on the ice every year. There are horse-sled races, tug-of-war contests (4) _____ different villages, and traditional Mongolian wrestling (5) _____. The wrestlers only wear shorts, boots, and a special jacket called a *zodog*, so only the toughest men try wrestling on the ice. I just watched.

Speaker 2

I'm a hotel receptionist. I've worked in hotels all around the world and made friends in different countries. When my friends got (1) _____, I was often invited to their wedding ceremonies. I've been very lucky to experience (2) _____ Chinese, Christian, Hindu, and Muslim weddings. Every culture and (3) _____ has different wedding (4) _____. For example, before Hindus get married, the bride has her hands covered with beautiful designs painted in a special ink called henna. This is called *mehndi*. And in Muslim weddings, it is traditional to give the bride and groom a boiled egg as a gift because it represents fertility and prosperity. But one thing is the same in every culture, after the (5) _____ there is always a big party!

UNIT 11 | *Why are they doing that?*

IV Speaking 1

Which of the following are important to you to experience on a trip? Check the boxes below and talk to your partner about what they think.

	Very important	Quite important	Not important	Reason
• religious events	☐	☐	☐	....
• traditional events	☐	☐	☐	....
• modern events	☐	☐	☐	....
• everyday life	☐	☐	☐	....
• local customs	☐	☐	☐	....
• _____	☐	☐	☐	....
• _____	☐	☐	☐	....

V Listening and Speaking 2

2-33

A Listen to the conversation and complete the text below.

Joseph: How was your trip to *Kathmandu*?

Amira: It was fantastic. I was there just at (1) _____ _____ _____ to *see the Indra Jātrā and Kumāri Jātrā festivals*.

Joseph: I don't know what **they are**. Can you (2) _____ _____ _____ **them**?

Amira: Sure. *They are religious festivals that last for eight days. In the Indra Jātrā, people dress up as gods and demons and dance along the streets.*

Joseph: Wow, that must be an (3) _____ thing to see.

Amira: It is. Then, *in the Kumāri Jātrā a big chariot with a goddess sitting on it is pulled through the streets. The goddess waved at me!*

Joseph: I (4) _____ _____ _____ you *saw a goddess*!

Amira: Yes. *Every few years a beautiful young girl is chosen to be the goddess.* The (5) _____ people said I was really lucky. It was an amazing (6) _____ .

B Now, practice the conversation with a partner.

C Next, change the information in *italics* using your own ideas and practice again.

69

VI Pronunciation

【 /b/ /p/ /v/ の発音 】

英語の学習者にとって、p と b、b と v の発音の違いが難しいと言われています。3 つの音の違いを確認しましょう。

/b/ の発音：唇を閉じた状態から少し強く息を押し出すように発音します。喉を振動させる有声音になります。　例）big /b/　been /b/

/p/ の発音：/b/ と同じく唇を閉じた状態から一気に息を外へ出すように発音します。喉を振動させない無声音です。　例）place /p/　people /p/

/v/ の発音：上の前歯で下唇に軽く触れながら、振動させるように発音します。
　　　　　　例）very /v/　never /v/

Exercises

A Listen to the words and choose the correct sound. 2-34

1. /b/ /p/ /v/　　　2. /b/ /p/ /v/　　　3. /b/ /p/ /v/
4. /b/ /p/ /v/　　　5. /b/ /p/ /v/　　　6. /b/ /p/ /v/

B Listen to the sentences and choose the correct sound. 2-35

1. /b/ /p/ /v/　　2. /b/ /p/ /v/　　3. /b/ /p/ /v/　　4. /b/ /p/ /v/

C Tongue Twister 2-36

"They both vied to buy the berry pie, but while I put the pan in the van, the pest in the best vest bought it for Betty, the very happy pet vet."

UNIT 11 | *Why are they doing that?*

VII Speaking 2

Find out about your classmates. Ask three people the following questions.

	Partner 1	Partner 2	Partner 3
1. What's your favorite cultural event?			
2. Does your hometown have a festival?			
3. Have you ever taken part in a local event?			
4. What's an event you want to see / take part in?			
5. What's a traditional custom you like?			
6. What's a custom in your country that you don't like?			
7. Do you like to wear traditional clothes?			
8. Your question: _____?			

memo

UNIT 12

It's delicious!

Local Food

I Vocabulary

A Match the English words and phrases (1~10) to the Japanese words (a~j).

1. ____ full board
2. ____ vegan
3. ____ allergy
4. ____ delicacy
5. ____ self-catering
6. ____ ingredients
7. ____ half board
8. ____ serve
9. ____ dishes
10. ____ vegetarian

a. 完全菜食主義者	b. 自炊の	c. 給仕をする
d. 一日二食付きの宿泊	e. 料理	f. おいしいもの
g. 一日三食付きの宿泊	h. 菜食主義者	i. 材料	j. アレルギー

B Complete the dialogs with words and phrases from Part A. 2-37~41

1. **A:** Does your hometown have a famous delicacy?
   B: Yes, it does. I'm from New Orleans and our most famous dish is jambalaya. The _____ are pork or chicken, sausage, rice, shrimp, green peppers, celery, chilli, and spices.
   A: Wow, that sounds delicious. Can you make it for me sometime?

2. **A:** What foods are seasonal right now?
   B: Well, it's summer, so fresh salads and cold _____ like *zarusoba* are popular.

3. **A:** Is there any food you can't eat?
   B: Yes, I have a(n) _____ to some seafood like shrimp and crab. If I eat any, I get very sick.

4. **A:** Are you a(n) _____?
   B: No, I'm not. I'm a vegetarian, so my diet is less strict. I eat things like cheese and eggs, and I love milk.

5. **A:** Would you ever go on a self-catering holiday?
   B: No, I wouldn't. When I go on vacation I just want to relax, not cook every day. I think the best choice for me is _____. That way I can enjoy breakfast and dinner at the hotel, and go to a different local restaurant every day for lunch.

C Practice the dialogs in Part B with a partner.

D Now, ask your partner the questions in Part B. Give your own responses.

II Listening and Speaking 1

2-42

A Listen to the questions and write them below.

1. _____
2. _____
3. _____
4. _____

B Now, select the best responses from the choices below.

1. **a.** Yes, I do.   **b.** Yes, I have.   **c.** Yes, I will.
2. **a.** Yes, when I'm busy.   **b.** Yes, it's my job.   **c.** Yes, I'd like to try it.
3. **a.** No, it's my job.   **b.** Yes, I have a reservation. **c.** I'm not sure.
4. **a.** I can't today.   **b.** No, but I'd like to.   **c.** Yes, let's go.

C Next, ask your partner the questions in Part A. Give your own responses.

III Listening

A Listen to two people talking about their food experiences. Write the places where they work/visited and check (O) the correct boxes.

1. Place: _____

	Yes	No
• works in a hotel	☐	☐
• chooses ingredients	☐	☐
• cooks meals	☐	☐
• writes a menu	☐	☐

2. Place: _____

	Yes	No
• works in a hotel	☐	☐
• chose ingredients	☐	☐
• cooked meals	☐	☐
• wrote a menu	☐	☐

B Listen to the speakers again. Complete the texts below.

Speaker 1

I'm the head chef at an international hotel in Chicago. We get guests from all over the world and that makes designing the room service menu a big (1) _____. Some guests are (2) _____ or vegan, so I have to include meat-free (3) _____ for them. Some religions have special rules about food, so I must make sure that the ingredients I use in my (4) _____ follow those rules. Finally, some people have food (5) _____, and I must be careful about using certain ingredients like nuts. Creating a menu that every guest can confidently order from is difficult, but I enjoy doing it and preparing the meals people order.

Speaker 2

Last year, I (1) _____ to try something different during my summer vacation. Usually, I stay in a big hotel and (2) _____ food from room service or go to the hotel restaurant. But this time, I decided to rent a (3) _____ apartment in a small village in France instead of going to a hotel. Every morning, I would walk to the bakery and buy freshly baked bread. Later, I would go to the town market and chat with local people while I (4) _____ fresh ingredients from the local farmers. Then, I would cook dinner with my family. It was a (5) _____ experience, and I can't wait to do it again.

UNIT 12 | It's delicious!

IV Speaking 1

Which of the following are important to you when choosing a restaurant on a trip?
Check the boxes below and talk to your partner about what they think.

	Very important	Quite important	Not important	Reason
• cost of the food	☐	☐	☐	....
• variety of dishes	☐	☐	☐	....
• serves local food	☐	☐	☐	....
• restaurant's popularity	☐	☐	☐	....
• restaurant reviews	☐	☐	☐	....
• _____	☐	☐	☐	....
• _____	☐	☐	☐	....

V Listening and Speaking 2

2-45

A Listen to the conversation and complete the text below.

Server: *Good evening.* May I help you?

Guest: *Yes, I don't have a reservation, but could I have a table for one please?*

Server: Just let me check. That's (1) _____ . Please come this way. I'll
(2) _____ _____ _____ menu.

Guest: Thank you. **What's the dish of the day?**

Server: Our (3) _____ delicacy. Paella made with fresh local seafood and (4) _____ with a seasonal salad and freshly baked bread.

Guest: (5) _____ _____ _____ . *I'd like to order that please.*

Server: Certainly. And what (6) _____ _____ _____ to drink?

Guest: *A glass of the house red wine,* please.

B Now, practice the conversation with a partner.

C Next, change the information in *italics* using your own ideas and practice again.

75

VI Pronunciation

【アクセントの位置】

英語のアクセントは母音の位置につき、いくつかルールがあります。アクセントの位置が正しくないと通じないことがあるので、基本的なルールを覚えておきましょう。

1. 接尾辞の1つ前の母音にアクセントがつくもの　-ious -ion -ian -ic など
   例）delicious　vegetarian（チェックがついているところにアクセントを付ける）
2. 接頭辞のすぐ後の母音にアクセントがつくもの　in- im- ad- un- en- con- など
   例）ingredients　enrich

Exercises

A Listen to the words and mark the correct stress using (✓).

1. extension　　2. connect　　3. important

4. instructor　　5. luxurious　　6. adventurer

B Listen to the sentences and mark the correct stress using (✓).

1. indeed　　2. precious　　3. impossible　　4. musician

C Tongue Twister

"The delicious dishes for greedy vegetarians are famous for their vegetable ingredients."

VII Speaking 2

Find out about your classmates. Ask three people the following questions.

	Partner 1	Partner 2	Partner 3
1. Does your hometown have a famous food, drink, or delicacy?			
2. What's your favorite food or drink?			
3. What's the strangest thing you have ever eaten?			
4. What's something you would never eat?			
5. What's your favorite restaurant?			
6. How often do you eat out?			
7. Are you allergic to any food or drink?			
8. Your question: _____?			

memo

UNIT 13

I don't feel good.
Medicine and Health

I Vocabulary

A Match the English words and phrases (1~10) to the Japanese words (a~j).

1. ____ sunburn
2. ____ fever
3. ____ medicine
4. ____ pharmacy
5. ____ emergency
6. ____ heart attack
7. ____ nausea
8. ____ chills
9. ____ diarrhea
10. ____ vaccination

a. 熱	b. 緊急事態	c. 日焼け	d. 予防接種	e. 薬局
f. 吐き気	g. 下痢	h. 寒気	i. 心臓発作	j. 薬

B Complete the dialogs with words and phrases from Part A. 2-49~53

1. **A:** Have you ever had a(n) _____ before traveling?
   B: Yes, I have. Before I went to Egypt, I got shots for hepatitis A, hepatitis B, typhoid, and yellow fever.

2. **A:** How are you feeling now?
   B: Better, thank you. That _____ has really helped my upset stomach. Both my nausea and diarrhea have stopped.

UNIT 13 *I don't feel good.*

3. **A:** Have you ever experienced a health _____?
   B: Yes, during a school trip, a student in my class had an epileptic seizure. It took everyone by surprise, and she had to be evacuated to a local hospital. She was fine, though. ［epileptic seizure　てんかん発作］

4. **A:** Have you ever had a(n) _____?
   B: Yes, I have. When I had influenza last year my temperature was 38.3°C.

5. **A:** Have you ever had a bad _____?
   B: No, I haven't. My skin is quite dark, so I just get a good tan instead.

C Practice the dialogs in Part B with a partner.

D Now, ask your partner the questions in Part B. Give your own responses.

II Listening and Speaking 1

2-54

A Listen to the questions and write them below.

1. _____
2. _____
3. _____
4. _____

B Now, select the best responses from the choices below.

1. **a.** Yes, I have.　　**b.** No, I didn't.　　**c.** Not this time.
2. **a.** Yes, every time.　**b.** Probably next year.　**c.** Maybe last year.
3. **a.** No, I didn't.　　**b.** No, I couldn't.　　**c.** No, I haven't.
4. **a.** Yes, it's here.　　**b.** It's over there.　　**c.** No, it's not near.

C Next, ask your partner the questions in Part A. Give your own responses.

III Listening

A Listen to two people talking about health problems. Write the problems they talk about and check (O) the correct boxes.

1. Problem: _____

	Yes	No
• is from Europe		
• skied for a week		
• visited a hospital		
• had sunburn		

2. Problem: _____

	Yes	No
• lives in Thailand		
• stayed in a hotel		
• had sunburn		
• helped a hotel guest		

B Listen to the speakers again. Complete the texts below.

Speaker 1

Three years ago, I went skiing in the Alps in Austria. It was my first time (1) _____ a European country, and I loved it. Unfortunately, after a couple of days of skiing my eyes became very (2) _____, and it was difficult to see anything. I was very worried, so I went to the local (3) _____. I had snow blindness, which happens when your eyes are sunburnt. I'm from Vietnam, so I was surprised to learn that you can get sunburn on a snowy (4) _____ in the winter! To get better I had to (5) _____ two days in a dark room.

Speaker 2

I have quite an (1) _____ job. I am a hotel doctor in Koh Chang, Thailand. I spend an (2) _____ a day at five different hotels. If any of the guests have health problems, they can come and see me. Most of the time, the problems my patients have are not (3) _____. Maybe they feel bad because they spent too much time in the sun, or they have an upset (4) _____ because they ate a new kind of food. But last year, a guest had a heart attack in one of the hotels. Luckily, he survived, but he had to be (5) _____ to the US.

80

UNIT 13 | I don't feel good.

IV Speaking 1

Which of the following are important to you when planning a trip? Check the boxes below and talk to your partner about what they think.

	Very important	Quite important	Not important	Reason
• dangerous animals	☐	☐	☐	
• dangerous weather	☐	☐	☐	
• good hospitals	☐	☐	☐	
• getting vaccinations	☐	☐	☐	
• health insurance	☐	☐	☐	
• _____	☐	☐	☐	
• _____	☐	☐	☐	

V Listening and Speaking 2

2-57

A Listen to the conversation and complete the text below.

Pharmacist: *Can I help you?*

Traveler: Yes, I need some (1) _____ for *my sunburn*.

Pharmacist: You **do look very red**. Can you tell me what (2) _____ ?

Traveler: I went *to the beach yesterday* and **fell asleep in the sun**.

Pharmacist: *How long were you sleeping in the sun?*

Traveler: *For about six hours*.

Pharmacist: Ah, I see. I can (3) _____ _____ _____ **cream for your sunburn**. But I think you (4) _____ probably (5) _____ _____ _____ to be safe. The hotel staff will be able to help you.

Traveler: Thank you. I'll ask them to (6) _____ _____ _____ for me today.

B Now, practice the conversation with a partner.

C Next, change the information in *italics* using your own ideas and practice again.

81

VI Pronunciation

【/ʌ/ /ɑ/ /e/ の発音】

英語の発音表記には、日本語の「あ」を連想させるものがいくつかあります。ここでは /ʌ/ と /ɑ/ の違いを確認しましょう。また、同じ母音である /e/ の発音も一緒に覚えましょう。

/ʌ/ の発音：唇をやや横に開き、短く発音します。カタカナの「アッ」に近い音です。
　　　　　例）upset /ʌ/　　cut /ʌ/

/ɑ/ の発音：唇をやや縦に開けて「オ」の形にして、カタカナの「ア」を発音するようなイメージです。　例）hospital /ɑ/　　box /ɑ/

/e/ の発音：唇を自然に開いて発音します。カタカナの「エ」とかなり近い音です。
　　　　　例）red /e/　　bed /e/

Exercises

A Listen to the words and choose the correct sound.　 2-58

1. /ʌ/ /ɑ/ /e/　　2. /ʌ/ /ɑ/ /e/　　3. /ʌ/ /ɑ/ /e/
4. /ʌ/ /ɑ/ /e/　　5. /ʌ/ /ɑ/ /e/　　6. /ʌ/ /ɑ/ /e/

B Listen to the sentences and choose the correct sound.　 2-59

1. /ʌ/ /ɑ/ /e/　　2. /ʌ/ /ɑ/ /e/　　3. /ʌ/ /ɑ/ /e/　　4. /ʌ/ /ɑ/ /e/

C Tongue Twister　 2-60

"Hey, John. Look at all the dead red bugs on and under the ugly box next to the bed."

UNIT 13 | *I don't feel good.*

VII Speaking 2

Find out about your classmates. Ask three people the following questions.

	Partner 1	Partner 2	Partner 3
1. Are you allergic to anything?			
2. Have you ever had a serious illness?			
3. Have you ever had a serious injury?			
4. What's your biggest health worry?			
5. What do you do to stay healthy?			
6. Do you worry about getting sick in a foreign country?			
7. If you got sick in a foreign country, what would you do?			
8. Your question: _____?			

memo

UNIT 14

How much is it?
Shopping

I Vocabulary

A Match the English words and phrases (1~10) to the Japanese words (a~j).

1. ____ discount
2. ____ try on
3. ____ normally
4. ____ reasonable
5. ____ gift-wrap
6. ____ tight
7. ____ negotiate
8. ____ sales tax
9. ____ unique
10. ____ afford

a. 交渉する　b. 独特の　c. 〜する余裕がある　d. きつい　e. 売上税
f. 試着する　g. 贈り物用に包装する　h. 通常　i. 割引き　j. 手ごろな

B Complete the dialogs with words and phrases from Part A.　2-61~65

1. **A:** Do you always buy souvenirs when you travel?
   B: No, not _____. I prefer going sightseeing to shopping.

2. **A:** I like your bag. How much was it?
   B: It was actually very _____, only ¥5,000. I'm so happy I bought it!

84

3. **A:** Have you ever asked for a(n) _____ at a shop?
   B: Yes. Once I bought a laptop computer that had been on display. I negotiated and got 10 percent off the price.

4. **A:** Do you prefer shopping at street markets or shopping malls?
   B: Shopping malls. It's easier to _____ clothes before buying them there.

5. **A:** Did you buy anything on your last vacation?
   B: No. I wanted to buy a new watch, but I couldn't _____ the one that I wanted. It was too expensive.

C Practice the dialogs in Part B with a partner.

D Now, ask your partner the questions in Part B. Give your own responses.

II Listening and Speaking 1

2-66

A Listen to the questions and write them below.

1. _____
2. _____
3. _____
4. _____

B Now, select the best responses from the choices below.

1. **a.** Family Mart is closest.   **b.** No, I don't like them.   **c.** It's not convenient to go.
2. **a.** Last time.   **b.** I was the first.   **c.** On Saturday.
3. **a.** There are many stores.   **b.** I shop elsewhere.   **c.** The local supermarket.
4. **a.** Yes, always.   **b.** Yes, sometimes.   **c.** It's heavy for me.

C Next, ask your partner the questions in Part A. Give your own responses.

III Listening  1-67,68

A Listen to two people talking about shops and shopping. Write the jobs they do and check (O) the correct boxes.

1. Job: _____

	Yes	No
• likes their job		
• can speak English		
• sells cold products		
• helps customers		

2. Job: _____

	Yes	No
• bought a key holder		
• sold a knife		
• spoke English		
• bought for a friend		

B Listen to the speakers again. Complete the texts below.

Speaker 1

I work at an airport, but I'm not a (1) _____ of security or one of the ground staff. I'm a sales clerk at a duty-free shop. The work is really (2) _____. There are lots of (3) _____ from all over the world and I often get to talk to them and practice my English. The products that we sell are cool, too. We sell a mix of traditional Japanese goods and (4) _____ items. I need to know a lot about the products so I can give advice to our customers, but I enjoy helping people decide what to buy. I hope that I've helped a lot of travelers get the (5) _____ souvenirs from their trips.

Speaker 2

I always buy souvenirs when I go traveling. But I was bored with always buying things like key holders and (1) _____ openers. So, when I went to Japan, I wanted to buy something unique. I'm a chef, so a friend (2) _____ getting a Japanese cooking knife. I thought that was a great idea, so I spent a day looking around the shops in Kappabashi, in Tokyo. There was a wide selection of knives, so it was difficult to (3) _____ one, but an English-speaking shop assistant (4) _____. The knife I bought was a bit expensive and I needed to pay sales tax, but it is really good (5) _____, and I even got my name engraved on it.

86

UNIT 14 | How much is it?

IV Speaking 1

Which of the following are important to you when buying a souvenir? Check the boxes below and talk to your partner about what they think.

	Very important	Quite important	Not important	Reason
• price	☐	☐	☐	
• uniqueness	☐	☐	☐	
• can negotiate	☐	☐	☐	
• gift-wrapping	☐	☐	☐	
• is traditional	☐	☐	☐	
• _____	☐	☐	☐	
• _____	☐	☐	☐	

V Listening and Speaking 2

2-69

A Listen to the conversation and complete the text below.

Customer: Hi. I'd (1) _____ _____ _____ on *this dress*. Can you tell me where the fitting rooms are, please?

Shop assistant: Sure. They're (2) _____ over there. I'll show you. [A little later] How **was it**?

Customer: *A little tight*. Do you have the same **dress**, but in a (3) _____?

Shop assistant: I'll (4) _____ _____ _____ for you. *No, I'm afraid we don't*.

Customer: Oh. *That's a shame*.

Shop assistant: Yes. Is (5) _____ _____ _____ I can help you with?

Customer: Well, I do like **this watch**. Can I pay for **it by credit card**?

Shop assistant: Yes, (6) _____. Would you like me to **gift-wrap it for you**?

Customer: No, that's fine. Thank you.

B Now, practice the conversation with a partner.

C Next, change the information in *italics* using your own ideas and practice again.

87

VI Pronunciation

《強弱の付け方》

英語で話すとき、強弱を付けてリズミカルに発音することが大切です。基本的に、名詞、be動詞以外の動詞、形容詞、副詞などを強く発音します。また、大事な内容は強く、それ以外は弱く発音します。

例) I <u>want</u> to <u>buy</u> a <u>new</u> <u>watch</u>. 下線部を強く発音してみましょう。

Exercises

A Listen to the sentences below and underline the stressed words. 2-70

1. He went to the art museum.
2. This shirt is so expensive.
3. You can see a beautiful beach.

B Listen to the sentences and write the words you hear. Then practice saying the sentences, paying attention to stress. 2-71

1. This _____ is _____ _____ the _____.
2. I'd _____ to _____ a _____ gift for a _____ occasion.

C Tongue Twister 2-72

"Betty Botter bought a bit of butter, but the butter Betty bought was bitter."

UNIT 14 | How much is it?

VII Speaking 2

Find out about your classmates. Ask three people the following questions.

	Partner 1	Partner 2	Partner 3
1. Do you like shopping?			
2. Where do you like to go shopping?			
3. Who do you like to go shopping with?			
4. What is the most expensive thing you've ever bought?			
5. Do you prefer online shopping or going to a store?			
6. What is something you would like to buy?			
7. Have you ever bought anything at a street market?			
8. Your question: _____?			

memo

UNIT 15

Where to next?

Reminiscing and Future Plans

I Vocabulary

A Match the English words and phrases (1~10) to the Japanese words (a~j).

1. ____ homestay
2. ____ island
3. ____ return
4. ____ during
5. ____ parasailing
6. ____ exchange student
7. ____ through
8. ____ journey
9. ____ graduate
10. ____ honeymoon

| a. 卒業する | b. パラセーリング | c. ハネムーン | d. 戻る | e. 留学生 |
| f. 旅行 | g. ホームステイ | h. ~を通して | i. 島 | j. ~の間 |

B Complete the dialogs with words and phrases from Part A. 2-73~77

1. **A:** How was your vacation?
   B: It was so romantic! We spent the first week of our _____ in Hawaii, and then we flew to California and spent a week staying at the Disneyland Resort.

2. **A:** What is the best thing about studying at this school?
   B: The school trips. In our second year, we did a(n) _____ in Rome for two weeks.

90

UNIT 15 **Where to next?**

3. **A:** What is the longest _____ you have ever been on?
   B: I once drove from Flagstaff, Arizona, to New York City. It took about 34 hours to travel there by car.

4. **A:** What are you going to do _____ the winter vacation?
   B: I'm going to spend five days skiing in Switzerland.

5. **A:** Who is that student over there?
   B: Do you mean the girl sitting next to Riko? That's Jane. She is our new _____ from New Zealand.

C Practice the dialogs in Part B with a partner.

D Now, ask your partner the questions in Part B. Give your own responses.

II Listening and Speaking 1

A Listen to the questions and write them below.

1. _____
2. _____
3. _____
4. _____

B Now, select the best responses from the choices below.

1. **a.** I went shopping.　　**b.** I went to England.　　**c.** No, I didn't.
2. **a.** Yes, every time.　　**b.** Yes, it really was.　　**c.** Yes, it is.
3. **a.** Yes, three times.　　**b.** Yes, she likes it.　　**c.** Yes, for my family.
4. **a.** Yes, Paris.　　**b.** No, I went two times.　　**c.** Yes, everyone does.

C Next, ask your partner the questions in Part A. Give your own responses.

III Listening 2-79,80

A Listen to two people talking about their travel experiences. Write the places they talk about and check (O) the correct boxes.

1. Place: _____

	Yes	No
• went with family		
• stayed in a hotel		
• swam in the sea		
• went parasailing		

2. Place: _____

	Yes	No
• loves anime		
• studied art		
• is a student		
• lives in Japan		

B Listen to the speakers again. Complete the texts below.

Speaker 1

I went to Langkawi in Malaysia with my family in (1) _____ last year. Langkawi is a (2) _____ of 99 islands next to Thailand, so the winter weather is still hot. We stayed in a hotel next to the beach. Langkawi has the most beautiful beaches I've ever seen! I (3) _____ in the sea every morning. My daughters were too (4) _____ to go swimming in the sea, so they played in the hotel pool (5) _____. I want to go back again this winter and watch the sun rise while parasailing.

Speaker 2

I spent a year in a Japanese high school as an (1) _____ student when I was sixteen. I was interested in all parts of Japanese (2) _____, but the reason I went to Japan was because I love manga and anime. I went back to Japan every summer vacation (3) _____ high school and university. I studied art at university, and I (4) _____ this year. Now I'm (5) _____ to go back to Japan again. I'm returning to Kyoto to work for an anime studio. It's my dream job.

92

UNIT 15 | *Where to next?*

IV Speaking 1

Which of the following are important to you when planning a trip? Check the boxes below and talk to your partner about what they think.

	Very important	Quite important	Not important	Reason
• the cost of the trip	☐	☐	☐	....
• travel time	☐	☐	☐	....
• things to see there	☐	☐	☐	....
• things to do there	☐	☐	☐	....
• safety	☐	☐	☐	....
• _____	☐	☐	☐	....
• _____	☐	☐	☐	....

V Listening and Speaking 2 2-81

A Listen to the conversation and complete the text below.

Steve: So, how was your first time (1) _____ *Paris*?

Kumiko: It was (2) _____! I'll never forget *the view of the city from the Eiffel Tower*. And the *food was incredible*!

Steve: It sounds great. I'm glad you had a good trip. Have you (3) _____ *where you will go* next year?

Kumiko: Actually, I've already (4) _____ _____ mind. I'm *going back to France*.

Steve: Really? (5) _____ _____! What's your plan?

Kumiko: I'm going to (6) _____ _____ *staying with a friend I made there*.

B Now, practice the conversation with a partner.

C Next, change the information in *italics* using your own ideas and practice again.

93

VI Pronunciation

> **【/ou/ と /u:/ の発音】**
>
> /ou/ は、口を丸くして強めに「オ」と発音してから、唇をすぼめながら弱めに「ウ」と発音します。
>
> 　例）h<u>o</u>mestay /ou/　　h<u>o</u>tel /ou/
>
> /u:/ は、唇を丸めて少し突き出し、「オ」と「ウ」の中間くらいの音を出します。/ou/ よりも伸ばして発音しましょう。
>
> 　例）p<u>oo</u>l /u:/　　tw<u>o</u> /u:/

Exercises

A Listen to the words and choose the correct sound.

1. /ou/　/u:/
2. /ou/　/u:/
3. /ou/　/u:/
4. /ou/　/u:/
5. /ou/　/u:/
6. /ou/　/u:/

B Listen to the sentences and choose the correct sound.

1. /ou/　/u:/
2. /ou/　/u:/
3. /ou/　/u:/
4. /ou/　/u:/

C Tongue Twister

"No soup, boots, rope, or soap in the school pool, only loads of boats and floats."

UNIT 15 | *Where to next?*

VII Speaking 2

Find out about your classmates. Ask three people the following questions.

	Partner 1	Partner 2	Partner 3
1. Where did you go on your last trip?			
2. What is your best summer vacation memory?			
3. Would you go on vacation to the same place more than once?			
4. Is there a sightseeing spot you want to visit again?			
5. How much time do you spend planning a trip?			
6. Where do you want to go next summer?			
7. Where do you want to go next winter?			
8. Your question: _____?			

memo

95

Appendix

Unit 1

Topic 1: Where shall we go?
— Choosing a Vacation

What do you think?

Choose one of the statements below. Prepare a short response giving your opinion.

- Active vacations are better than relaxing vacations.
- We should take vacations in our own country rather than going abroad.

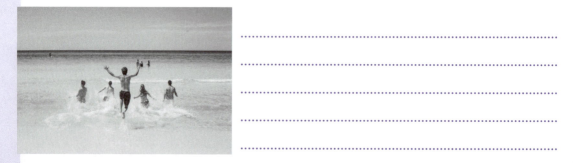

Unit 2

Topic 2: **Just click there.**
– Booking a Vacation

What do you think?

Choose one of the statements below. Prepare a short response giving your opinion.

- Booking vacations online is best.
- We should always read reviews of a hotel before booking a room.

....
....
....
....
....

Unit 3

Topic 3: **Let's get ready.**
– Packing and Preparing

What do you think?

Choose one of the statements below. Prepare a short response giving your opinion.

- Good preparation is the most important part of having a good vacation.
- Preparing and packing early is best.

....
....
....
....
....

Unit 4

Topic 4: Which gate?
  – At the Airport
     (Departing)

What do you think?

Choose one of the statements below. Prepare a short response giving your opinion.

- Checking in online is better than checking in at a counter.
- Airport parking should be free.

....
....
....
....
....

Unit 5

Topic 5: Where are the taxis?
  – At the Airport (Arriving)

What do you think?

Choose one of the statements below. Prepare a short response giving your opinion.

- All airports should have English signs.
- Countries should have more relaxed customs rules.

....
....
....
....
....

Unit 6

Topic 6: Welcome!
– Checking In

What do you think?

Choose one of the statements below. Prepare a short response giving your opinion.

- Hotel front desks should be replaced with automated check-in machines.
- Staying with local people is better than staying in a hotel.

....
....
....
....
....

Unit 7

Topic 7: This isn't right.
– Resolving Problems

What do you think?

Choose one of the statements below. Prepare a short response giving your opinion.

- Hotel guests that have problems should be given compensation.
- Resolving problems is the most important part of a hotel worker's job.

....
....
....
....
....

Unit 8

Topic 8: Let's work out.
– Hotel Facilities and Services

What do you think?

Choose one of the statements below. Prepare a short response giving your opinion.

- All hotel facilities should be free for hotel guests.
- Ordering hotel room service is a waste of money.

....
....
....
....
....

Unit 9

Topic 9: Where's the station?
– Getting Around Town

What do you think?

Choose one of the statements below. Prepare a short response giving your opinion.

- Taking a tour is the best way to experience a new city.
- Using smartphones for directions means we sometimes miss interesting places.

....
....
....
....

Unit 10

Topic 10: Look at that!
– Sights and Tourist Spots

What do you think?

Choose one of the statements below. Prepare a short response giving your opinion.

- Group tours are better than exploring a city alone.
- Just visiting famous sights and tourist spots is boring.

....
....
....
....
....

Unit 11

Topic 11: Why are they doing that?
– Local Culture

What do you think?

Choose one of the statements below. Prepare a short response giving your opinion.

- Understanding foreign cultures can help us to understand our own culture better.
- We should try to preserve traditional customs and events.

....
....
....
....
....

Unit 12

Topic 12: It's delicious!
– Local Food

What do you think?

Choose one of the statements below. Prepare a short response giving your opinion.

- Trying local delicacies is an important part of traveling abroad.
- It is better to eat familiar food when we travel abroad.

Unit 13

Topic 13: I don't feel good.
– Health Problems

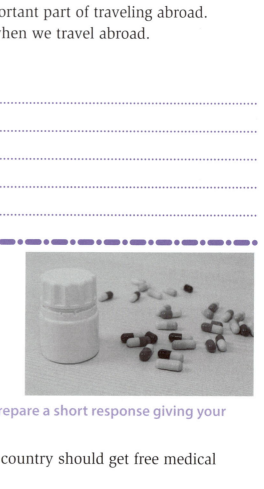

What do you think?

Choose one of the statements below. Prepare a short response giving your opinion.

- People who get sick in a foreign country should get free medical treatment.
- There are some countries we shouldn't visit because we might get sick.

Unit 14

Topic 14: How much is it?
– Shopping

What do you think?

Choose one of the statements below. Prepare a short response giving your opinion.

- Shopping for souvenirs is a waste of time.
- We should only buy souvenirs that have been made by local people.

....
....
....
....
....

Unit 15

Topic 15: Where to next?
– Reminiscing and Future Plans

What do you think?

Choose one of the statements below. Prepare a short response giving your opinion.

- It is better to visit one place many times than to always go somewhere new.
- We should try to experience as many different places as we can.

....
....
....
....
....

103

TEXT PRODUCTION STAFF

edited by / 編集
Minako Hagiwara / 萩原 美奈子

cover design by / 表紙デザイン
Nobuyoshi Fujino / 藤野 伸芳

CD PRODUCTION STAFF

narrated by / 吹き込み者
Howard Colefield (AmE) / ハワード・コルフィールド（アメリカ英語）
Karen Haedrich (AmE) / カレン・ヘドリック（アメリカ英語）

Where to Next? – Travel and Tourism Communication
観光・海外旅行のための英語コミュニケーション演習

2025年1月20日　初版発行
2025年2月15日　第2刷発行

著　者　James Bury
　　　　Anthony Sellick
　　　　堀内 香織

発行者　佐野 英一郎

発行所　株式会社 成 美 堂
　　　　〒101-0052　東京都千代田区神田小川町3-22
　　　　TEL 03-3291-2261　FAX 03-3293-5490
　　　　https://www.seibido.co.jp

印刷・製本　萩原印刷株式会社

ISBN 978-4-7919-7307-1　　　　Printed in Japan

・落丁・乱丁本はお取り替えします。
・本書の無断複写は、著作権上の例外を除き著作権侵害となります。